D1713955

# Ori

*The Ultimate Guide to Spiritual Intuition, Yoruba, Odu, Egbe, Orishas, and Ancestral Veneration*

© Copyright 2023 - All rights reserved.

The content contained within this book may not be reproduced, duplicated, or transmitted without direct written permission from the author or the publisher.

Under no circumstances will any blame or legal responsibility be held against the publisher, or author, for any damages, reparation, or monetary loss due to the information contained within this book, either directly or indirectly.

**Legal Notice:**

This book is copyright protected. It is only for personal use. You cannot amend, distribute, sell, use, quote or paraphrase any part, or the content within this book, without the consent of the author or publisher.

**Disclaimer Notice:**

Please note the information contained within this document is for educational and entertainment purposes only. All effort has been executed to present accurate, up-to-date, reliable, and complete information. No warranties of any kind are declared or implied. Readers acknowledge that the author is not engaging in the rendering of legal, financial, medical, or professional advice. The content within this book has been derived from various sources. Please consult a licensed professional before attempting any techniques outlined in this book.

By reading this document, the reader agrees that under no circumstances is the author responsible for any losses, direct or indirect, that are incurred as a result of the use of the information contained within this document, including, but not limited to, errors, omissions, or inaccuracies.

# Your Free Gift
# (only available for a limited time)

Thanks for getting this book! If you want to learn more about various spirituality topics, then join Mari Silva's community and get a free guided meditation MP3 for awakening your third eye. This guided meditation mp3 is designed to open and strengthen ones third eye so you can experience a higher state of consciousness. Simply visit the link below the image to get started.

https://spiritualityspot.com/meditation

# Table of Contents

# Introduction

At the start of this book, you'll be introduced to the fascinating background of the Yoruba religion. You'll learn how this belief system incorporates elements of art, religious and divinatory practices, and the myths and beliefs passed down through oral traditions. One of the fundamental beliefs of the Yoruba revolves around the concept of Ori. The term Ori is roughly translated to "destiny." However, as you'll learn later on, for the Yoruba, the meaning of Ori goes far beyond that. It's a means to spiritual elevation, a tool for developing one's intuition and using it to fulfill one's destiny - or change it if needed. That said, the concept of Ori contradicts another crucial element of the Yoruba beliefs, free will. To comprehend this conundrum, you'll need to understand how each component of Ori works together and how they relate to freedom of choice.

Through the intricate tales of the Yoruba, you'll learn how Ori was created and how Olodumare affects one's expression of it. As the supreme creator, Olodumare oversees all living beings and spirits, including the Orishas. The Yoruba venerate Orishas as deities and use them as spiritual messengers. Through spiritual communication, people can learn how to align their life and values with their Ori or intuition. It's believed that the Orishas can also contribute to how the Ori is expressed and how it affects one's life. According to a Yoruba myth, Ori can also be worshiped as an Orisha. As there are Orishas with different tastes, so there are different Oris that can be nurtured through a broad range of ways. Prayers, rituals, and offerings to one's spiritual intuition often go a long way toward healthy self-realization, which is sacred to the Yoruba.

Ancestral veneration is another practice that influences Yoruba beliefs and traditions. Ancestors play a crucial part in the life of the Yoruba. Their spirit can be evoked and asked for protection, guidance, and spiritual enlightenment through the wisdom the ancestors have gathered throughout their life. Consequently, the ancestors can help improve one's spiritual intuition and alignment with Ori. You'll also learn about another spiritual group that can assist you in this quest, the *Egbe Orun*. The Egbe are heavenly spirits who live in intricate societies and have their own characters and influences over human lives. Their impact results from their connection with the souls inhabiting the Earth.

Another way to ensure spiritual realizations is by living a righteous life. According to the Yoruba beliefs, this is only possible by following the _16 Truths of Ifa_, the decree created by Olodumare to help solve common issues people encounter throughout their lives. Last but not least, the book will remind you that the alignment of Ori depends mostly on you. While the spiritual entities mentioned in the previous chapters are certainly helpful to balance your Ori, in the end, it all comes down to your character. You'll be much closer to fulfilling your destiny or changing it by improving your character. This book will guide you through all the practices that contribute to self-realization through Ori. It provides a great stepping stone for those wanting to live a harmonious life by combining free will with fate. If you are ready to delve into the world of spiritual alignment through spirit guides and self-awareness, keep reading.

# Chapter 1: Basic Spiritual Concepts of Yoruba

The Yoruba faith is one of the largest religions in West Africa, mainly Nigeria. It is estimated to be 5000 years old, making it one of the oldest religions in the world, even predating Christianity. Yoruba has a huge following, with about one hundred million believers in Africa and other countries worldwide. It is based on various African beliefs, songs, proverbs, myths, and legends. In the Yoruba religion, Olodumare is the supreme deity and the creator of the universe who doesn't have a specific gender and is referred to using the pronoun "they." They aren't involved in the matters of mankind, so they created the Orishas (spirits and demigods) to assist human beings in their affairs. The spirits of the ancestors also play a big role in the Yoruba faith. Worshipers believe that the spirits of their dead family members live on after death. The Orishas and the spirits of the ancestors are highly revered in the Yoruba religion. They provide assistance, are a source of inspiration, and protect people from evil.

Yoruba has over one million followers worldwide.
https://www.pexels.com/photo/photo-of-woman-lighting-the-candlesticks-6192006/

Like many other religions at the time, Yoruba was passed down orally from one generation to the next. In many ancient cultures, illiteracy was common, which is why they didn't have any written records. Many cultures wrote down and preserved their myths and legends when literacy began spreading. However, since these stories were passed down orally, many have drifted from the original source, and there can be more than one version of the same story. For instance, Olodumare goes by many names in different legends, like Olofin and Olodumare-Oloorun. Some stories paint Olodumare as an absent deity who isn't involved in mankind's affairs. They live far away in the heavens, unable to hear the people's prayers. While other stories claim that Olodumare is an all-knowing deity who knows everything that goes on in Heaven and on Earth.

In the Yoruba hierarchy, no one is more significant than Olodumare:

- Olodumare
- The Orishas and the Ajogun
- Mankind
- The spirits of the ancestors
- Animals and plants

The Ajogn are supernatural entities that share similarities with the concept of the Devil in Christianity. Just like evil spirits, these beings bring many misfortunes to human beings, like disease, accidents, and many other troubles. At the same time, they encourage mayhem and chaos like the devil. However, one can't label Ajogn evil or put them in the same category as demons. In the Yoruba religion, no human or supernatural being is considered all good or all evil. Good and bad exist in every creature, even the Ajogn. This applies to the Orishas as well, who can commit mischief. It is a fair and realistic conception of the world since nothing can be considered perfect or entirely flawed.

Interestingly, the spirits of the ancestors fall under human beings in the hierarchy, even though their influence is obvious in the Yoruba religion. However, these spirits can only exert their powers through human veneration and acknowledgment, which is probably why they fall under them. Last on the hierarchy are animals and plants. However, this doesn't make them any less significant than mankind or the spirits of the ancestors. All creatures possess the spirit of the divine, which makes them all of equal value and influence. Therefore, all human beings are also connected since they share the spirit of the divine. Neither people's skin color, culture, nor religion can set them apart. We all share a link with one another and all living things.

The Yoruba people believe in destiny or *Ori*, which each person must achieve before death. The Orishas and the spirits of the ancestors help people realize their destinies. However, if one dies before they fulfill their Ori, they can try again in the next life. Death is considered a happy occasion that people should celebrate. Reincarnation supports this belief as it is something people look forward to instead of dreading. The Yoruba people don't believe that death is the end. Reincarnation or Atunwa is a prominent concept in their faith. It is the belief that the spirit can continue its cycle even after the body dies by coming back in different physical forms. This concept exists in many religions, like Buddhism and Hinduism. However, it is different in Yoruba since it takes place within the family. For instance, a grandfather can come back as his grandson. However, gender doesn't play a role here. Male spirits can come back in female physical forms and vice versa. When the spirit is reborn, it carries with it the wisdom and knowledge of its ancestor.

Life and death aren't regarded as opposites or a beginning and end, but the spirit goes through an ongoing cycle from one physical form to another. Reincarnation is a gift that is bestowed on mankind. However, only the spirits of good people who lead an honorable life can experience rebirth. Cruel people who harm gods' creatures aren't given this gift. Living a good and happy life is an essential part of the Yoruba faith, unlike some religions where one must suffer in this life to get rewarded in the next.

Yoruba had found its way into many other countries and cultures worldwide during the time of enslavement when black people were brought to the Americas. Although they were pressured to convert to Catholicism privately, they held onto their beliefs and combined their Orishas with Catholic saints. Yoruba wasn't just a religion. It represented their identity that they weren't willing to compromise on. Holding on to it was an act of defiance against a new culture that wanted to erase its history and beliefs.

There are many festivals in the Yoruba religion that celebrate Olodumare, the Orishas, and the spirits of the ancestors. They present offerings and reenact some of their famous myths and legends. All worshipers must participate in these festivals, or it will be considered an insult to the Orishas, spirits, and gods.

Different tribes and people have their own ways of celebrating the Orishas.
https://www.pexels.com/photo/women-of-massai-tribe-11679893/

The priests and priestesses have a significant and influential role in the Yoruba faith. Priests are called Babalawo, which is a Yoruba word that translates to "father of the mysteries." They lead all the religious ceremonies. When invoking an Orisha during a ritual, the spirit usually mounts the priest or priestess. Mounting is a form of possession that isn't forceful or bad like demonic possession.

On the contrary, it is an honor for the host. Attendees can then ask the Orisha for guidance and enlightenment. Suppose an Orisha possesses someone who isn't a priest or priestess. In that case, it is a sign that this person should be initiated into the priesthood. The Babalawos also perform divination for the chiefs or kings of Yoruba and provide spiritual consultation.

A priest or priestess must first initiate people who want to practice this religion. After initiation, they must follow certain rules and guidelines, including venerating the Orishas and refraining from eating pork. During initiation, an Orisha chooses someone to guide and help fulfill their destiny.

The Yoruba guidelines are:

1. One can change their destiny except for the day they are born, and the day they will die.
2. Each person is a part of the universe (this isn't figurative but intended in the literal sense).
3. One must lead a successful, fulfilled, and happy life.
4. One should never harm nature.
5. One must acquire knowledge and wisdom throughout their life.
6. Each person is born with a destiny, and they must live through it.
7. One is born from their blood relatives.
8. One must never harm another person.
9. One must work with their worldly and spiritual self.
10. One must fear nothing.
11. Heaven is one's real home, while the physical world is the marketplace, and the human spirit is constantly journeying between the two.
12. There is no Devil.
13. The spirits of the ancestors must be revered.
14. The Orishas are a part of each person.
15. There is only one chief deity.

About 20% of the people of Yoruba practice the religion. Even those who converted to Christianity or Islam still hold on to some aspects of the Yoruba religion their ancestors practiced.

# Santeria

Santeria is a religion that originated from Yoruba in South and Latin America and in parts of the United States. Santeria is a Spanish word that translates to *"the way of the saints."* The religion goes by other names as well, like La Religión Lucumí, which is Spanish for *"the order of Lucumí,"* and La Regla de Ocha, which is also Spanish and translates to *"the order of the Orishas."*

In the 19th century, Santeria made its way to Brazil, Cuba, Puerto Rico, Haiti, and Trinidad through the slave trade. The religion found its way to the U.S. in the 20th century. From 1959, after the Cuban revolution, and until the 21st century, about one million Cubans immigrated to the U.S. and other countries in South America, where they spread their religious practices. It wasn't just people of African descent who were interested in Santeria – but Latin and white Americans as well. Even those who didn't adopt the religion's traditions were still curious about the concept of the Orishas. It is believed that millions of people sought their help at one point in their lives.

However, before Santeria became widely accepted, worshippers practiced their faith in secret to avoid punishment. Therefore, people couldn't keep records of their faith for centuries and passed down all information orally from one generation to the next. Things changed after the Cuban revolution as the government openly acknowledged Santeria and its followers didn't need to hide. However, it still remains an oral tradition.

There were some concerns among the Cuban government that Santeria could be associated with witchcraft. However, this didn't stop people from showing interest in the religion. In the 1980s, many people were initiated into Santeria, and its popularity hasn't slowed since. About 80% of the Cuban people either follow Santeria or practice some of its traditions.

During enslavement, the African people found that they could only practice their religion by combining some of their Orishas with Catholic saints, hence the name Santeria. However, some disagree with the idea that both religions merged together. The Afro-Cuban people didn't find the need to blend the two but followed both religions simultaneously as they found many similarities between them. Many Santeria followers have converted and adapted to Catholicism. They baptize their children and go to church while still practicing Santeria tradition in their homes and temples. They don't feel the need to give up one faith to practice another as they see the parallelism between the two.

There aren't many differences between Yoruba and Santeria. In Santeria, Oldumare also created the universe, and the Orishas greatly influenced mankind and their daily lives. Santeria is based on the relationship devotees develop with the Orishas. It is a mutually beneficial relationship where worshipers venerate the Orishas and receive their blessings in return. The followers of Santeria also believe in the concept of Ori and that Olodumare grants every person a destiny they must fulfill.

Anyone can follow Santeria, no matter what their background or age. During initiation, people are asked to dress all in white. Those who want to follow Santeria must agree to live according to the way of the Orishas or *la regla de ocha*. There are certain rules that they must follow during the initiation process, which can last up to a year. For instance, they aren't allowed to leave the house at night for a whole year. They can't touch or let anyone touch them unless they are their partners or family members, and they should only wear white attire. All Santeria rituals, including initiation, take place in public or at home since there aren't any temples. Since it is an oral tradition, rites and ceremonies are a big part of the religion as it allows devotees to share and pass down the stories and practices.

Santeria has become a diverse religion, with people from different backgrounds and cultures practicing it. However, it is still identified as an Afro-Cuban religion.

# Voodoo

Voodoo has always been associated with black magic, evil spirits, demons, and evil. This is an unfair representation of the faith that has been spread by pop culture. Like Yoruba and Santeria, Voodoo is a religious belief that isn't associated with witchcraft. This misconception stems from some misinterpretations linked to Voodoo for centuries. Hollywood has also played a part in creating a false image of the faith and associating it with cannibalism, torture, and devil worship. The misunderstandings began in the late 18th century when witnesses misinterpreted a Voodoo ritual and thought the people were making a deal with the devil.

Voodoo is one of the oldest religions in the world.
*https://unsplash.com/photos/7PWISrkiPW4*

Voodoo, also spelled Vodoun and Vodou, originated in Haiti and found its way to America through the slave trade. The followers of Voodoo are called Vodouisants, and many reside in New Orleans, Haiti, and different parts of the Caribbean. It is one of the oldest religions in the world, as it is believed to be 6000 years old. Modern Voodoo is different from its ancient practices as it has blended with African traditions, magic, and Catholicism. However, Voodoo is a dynamic religion that isn't governed by a set of rules. It is so flexible that two temples in the same town can practice completely different traditions.

There are common patterns among the traditions of Voodoo as the Yoruba religion heavily influenced it. For instance, Voodoo's followers venerate their ancestors' spirits and worship spirits similar to the Orishas called Lwas. Their rituals usually involve dancing and playing drums. Lwas serve the same purpose as the Orishas, acting as intermediaries between the Voodoo supreme deity Bondye and mankind. Humans present offerings to the Lwas, and they provide assistance in return. They exist with the spirits of the dead in a place called Vilokan. Voodoo is a monotheistic religion which is the belief in only one god, Bondye. The name is derived from two French words, *bon dieu,* which translates to "good god."

The Vodouisants use Voodoo dolls in their religious practices. However, they don't cause any harm. The dolls are mainly used to venerate Lwas. Voodoo also shares many similarities with Catholicism, like prayers and using candles.

# Candomblé

Candomblé, originally called Batuque, is another religion borrowed from Catholicism and African traditions like Yoruba. The word Candomblé means *"dance in honor of the gods."* Over two million people from many countries, like Brazil, practice Candomblé. They believe that there are multiple deities, with each having its own responsibilities and powers. The concept of destiny is also prominent here, and the gods assist people in pursuing and fulfilling their destinies.

In the last few centuries, the religion has gained many followers in Brazil and other countries. However, Candomblé was outlawed for a very long time, and the Catholic Church prosecuted all its practitioners. The Church feared the growing popularity of Candomblé since it was associated with slave revolts and pagan practices. In the 1970s, things changed, and practicing Candomblé became legal again in Brazil.

Unlike the Abrahamic religions, Candomblé doesn't have sacred texts like the Bible or the Quran. It is an oral religion similar to other African-based beliefs. The followers of Candomblé, like Yoruba, believe in the supreme deity Olodumare and Orishas. However, Candomblé's beliefs differ from one region to another. Therefore, there are several variations of this religion.

Followers of Candomblé believe in reincarnation, which is why the bodies of their dead aren't allowed to be cremated. Although they believe in life after death, religion isn't concerned with the concept of the afterlife. Ori or destiny has a major role in the Candomblé faith, and each person must fulfill their own. Some destines are ethical, where the people lead an honorable life, while there are unethical destinies, where a person does harm to themselves and others. However, unethical actions have consequences. People learn about their destinies from the spirits of their ancestors. During a ritual, the spirit mounts (or possesses) the priest or priestess, and attendees can ask them about their destiny.

Priestesses play a bigger role in Candomblé than priests as they run Candomblé temples with the help of a priest. Priestesses are ialorixá - which means *"mothers of saints,"* and priests are called babalorixá -

which means *"fathers of saints."* Ialorixá also serve as healers and fortune tellers in their community. Followers of Candomblé can practice their religion at home or in temples. One must follow certain rules before entering a temple, like wearing clean clothes.

# Umbanda

Umbanda is another Brazilian religion that is based on African beliefs. The religion was first practiced in Brazil in the 19th century. It spread to other countries in South America, like Uruguay and Argentina. It is estimated that half a million people practice Umbanda in Brazil. However, it is believed that the number could be much bigger as many people don't practice it in public. The Umbanda followers worship the supreme deity Olodumareb, but they refer to them as Zambia and highly revere the Orishas.

The Umbanda followers revere the spirits of their ancestors, who they call Preto Velho (the old black man) and Preta Velha (the old black woman). These are the spirits of the people who died during enslavement. These spirits are kind-hearted, compassionate, and forgiving. Baianos is another influential spirit. They are also the spirits of the ancestors, mainly of the dead Umbanda practitioners.

Umbanda rituals involve communicating with the spirits of the ancestors, dancing, chanting, and drumming. During rituals, all practitioners must wear white and be barefoot at all times. Shoes have no place in Umbanda rituals since they are unclean.

When slaves were brought from Africa to the new world, they couldn't bring many of their possessions with them. They lost their families, homes, and freedom. The only thing that no one could take away from them was their identity. The African religions represented who they were and what they believed in. For this reason, they brought their beliefs, stories, and songs with them. They were the only things that reminded them of home. Years later, these religions are still influential not only in the lives of the African people but on people from different cultures and backgrounds.

# Chapter 2: What Is Ori?

In the Yoruba language, the word "Ori" means "head." However, the literal translation doesn't do justice to what this concept signifies. According to Yoruba cosmology, Ori represents human consciousness, a part of one's body and soul. And it connects the people to the supreme deity Olodumare. This connection is similar to the umbilical cord, which connects a mother with her child. Therefore, it is how one can connect and communicate with Olodumare. Since Olodumare is the creator of everything and exists in everyone, an Ori can be a symbol of the deity who breathed life into all living things.

Even though the literal translation of ori is 'head', it actually represents human consciousness.
https://commons.wikimedia.org/wiki/File:African_mask_(3146098034).jpg

It is essential to note that Ori doesn't represent destiny itself but rather its structure. It is considered the arbiter of one's destiny. The concept of destiny, or Ayanmo, is one of the components of Ori. An Ori is a map that plans out the road each person will take in their life. The concept of Ori is connected to the idea of fate or destiny. It is the essence of each person, their true nature, and every individual has their own unique Ori.

Its association with the divine is what makes it sacred. It is more than just the physical head that contains one's brain. It's where the inner spiritual self exists. An Ori is also the essence of who you are. It is the personality that defines you and the main force behind all your actions. It is what drives your thoughts and emotions. If you want to learn about your true nature, understand your Ori. People who have an identity crisis or complain about not knowing who they are, need to dig deep within themselves, peel all the layers, and come face to face with their inner selves. The Yoruba people describe the Ori as a spirit, and its power lies between Olodumare and human beings. Hence, it can be its own entity, an Orisha.

Orishas are supernatural entities that were created by Olodumare. When they created the universe, they realized that the human brain was too simple to grasp the concept of such a powerful deity. Therefore, they would not be able to directly interact with human beings. They created the Orishas to assist in mankind's affairs. One of the Orishas' purposes is to help and guide mankind to realize their destiny. They can also bring balance and alignment between one's physical and spiritual aspects of self. Thus, achieving an alignment with one's Ori as well.

The Yoruba people believe that before each person is born, they choose their own destiny, like where they will live, who they will fall in love with, how many children they will have, and even how they will die. They describe it as each person kneeling in heaven in front of Orunmila, the Orisha of divinity, and choosing their destiny with Orunmila's approval. Olodumare then seals the chosen Oris, and they are kept away as no one is allowed to interfere or alter them. This means that every person chooses how they will live their life. However, when a person is born, they forget their Ori and spend their lives trying to remember it and fulfill it.

Since each person chooses their own destiny, they are responsible for the type of life they will lead. Choosing a good Ori guarantees one will live a happy and easy life where one can achieve all their goals. In other words, a good Ori is an equivalent of being "lucky," where someone can have everything they want. They marry their soulmate, have a fulfilling career, live in their dream homes, have good health and great kids, and become wealthy. Everything they touch turns to gold, and everything they want, they can have. The concept of the Ori explains why some people lead happy and successful lives while others struggle. All the big and influential events in a person's life, like having a special talent, becoming wealthy, or dying young, are all attributed to one's Ori.

Having bad or imperfect Oris will lead to a hard and unhappy life where one will only experience bad luck. They will struggle to achieve their goals and will suffer for most of their lives. However, one's Ori isn't fixed, and one can change things for themselves to repair their destiny. Whenever one feels down on their luck and nothing seems to go their way, or if one feels lost and is looking for answers as to what they should be doing with their lives, this means that their Ori requires appeasing. Certain rituals and sacrifices can bring a great transformation, alter one's destiny for the best, and bring balance and alignment to one's spiritual life. You will notice a change when you achieve alignment with your Ori. Positivity will replace the negativity in your life, you'll be satisfied, and you'll achieve fulfillment and inner peace.

This begs the question, do people choose bad Oris? If you control your destiny, how do so many people end up failing and suffering in life? Choosing a good Ori doesn't guarantee that you'll lead a happy life. How a person employs their Ori in both its meanings (head and destiny) is what determines if one fails or succeeds in life. For instance, if you choose an Ori to become a doctor but don't study medicine, you will not fulfill your destiny and may be unhappy as a result. Being a good person can also impact your Ori. Whether your Ori is perfect or flawed, you can never realize it without a good character.

"Ori gbe eni naa" is a very popular saying among the Yoruba people, and it translates to "One's head can make him prosperous." While another proverb says, "Ori eni naa gba'bode," which means "One's head brought disappointment." The two sayings showcase the significance of one's Ori in determining what kind of life one will lead. According to the Yoruba people, those who fail to take advantage of their Ori are deemed fools.

Orunmila, the Orisha of wisdom and knowledge, can fix and change one's Ori. His influence in changing one's destiny was mentioned in Yoruba mythology. One of their prayer poems describes Orunmila as the savior of the less fortunate as he can change the Ori or the destiny of those who will die young. The poem mentions that he has the knowledge and wisdom to fix a bad Ori and change the course of people's lives.

Choosing your destiny proves that all these powerful beings like Olodumare and the Orishas have no control over one's destiny, indicating that the Yoruba people believe in free will. One's Ori can be interpreted as their own god who governs the person's life under the supervision of the divine, who doesn't control or meddle with mankind's destiny – but simply observes. Olodumare, with all their power, can't interfere and changes one's Ori. The deity's involvement in mankind's lives is non-existent. Although some stories describe Olodumare as a deity who is there for their creation, they still don't impact a person's Ori. Even Orunmila would not interfere in one's Ori unless he was invoked and asked to.

Each person must be born with an Ori. If a person doesn't have a destiny, there would be no point in their existence. They would have nothing to live for or achieve. When the Olodumare created mankind, they gave each person their own Ori so they could live the life they wanted and accomplish all their goals.

Since people forget their Oris after birth, they neglect the concept altogether and lose the connection they once shared with their destiny. *Your Ori isn't a stranger!* You made its acquaintance before you came out of your mother's womb or took your first breath. Reconnect with it once again by acknowledging it and showing it love and devotion. Ask it for blessings and good fortune, and pray that your Ori will give you a good day every morning. Make connecting with it a part of your daily routine to ensure an alignment with your destiny and a deeper understanding of yourself. Treat your Ori as a friend and talk to it whenever you feel alone. Open up to it, and don't be afraid to show it your most vulnerable self.

Obatala, the sky father and the Orisha who created human beings, molded the human head from clay. Thus, he was responsible for creating the human consciousness. Obatala didn't use magical powers to create the Oris. He molded each one by hand like an artist. Therefore, not all Oris look the same. Like any work of art, some will be perfect, while others can be flawed. In the myth of creation in Yoruba mythology, one time, when Obatala was molding human beings, he got drunk and ended up creating deformed people. Guilty and ashamed, Obalata vowed never to drink again, and he became the protector of the deformed.

When an individual chooses their Ori, they aren't just picking a destiny but also a specific pattern of energy to provide assistance and guidance to the consciousness during reincarnation. This energy pattern – which is also referred to as a spiritual force - helps the person's Ori or consciousness during reincarnation. This helpful spiritual force can also refer to one's personal Orisha since each person should have their own spirit to help them realize their Ori. In time, after the spirit experiences multiple reincarnations, the person's Ori or consciousness will expand due to the wisdom and knowledge they get with every reincarnation.

# Ori Arena of Perception

The Yoruba people believe that four arenas of perception function as one's Ori. They are all governed by consciousness hence their association with the Ori.

- The first one is described as "identity emotions," which one uses to reflect on their internal experience when encountering a new one.

- Assess how a new experience can impact your relationship with others and your level of empathy toward them, as well

- Accessing one's memory to reminisce about similar past experiences

- Imagining the impact of the experience on the future

Throughout the day, one experiences these four modes. It is how the brain takes in and processes information. Whenever one encounters a new experience, one evaluates its impact on their emotions, which can bring up similar experiences and feelings from the past. Then they assess the impact the experience has on their current relationships and the consequences of this experience in the future. In Yoruba mythology, how a person perceives the information can heavily impact their personality. The Yoruba people have a saying that you leave your home as someone in the morning and come back at night as a different person.

Being connected with the spiritual aspect of one's self makes a person aware of how they process new information and experiences. By employing the Ori or consciousness, they can expand their perception of the world and how they live through their personal experiences.

Ori isn't only significant as one's destiny but also as their consciousness. Without Ori, you would be unable to interpret human experiences, understand, or process any new information.

# Types of Ori

In Yoruba mythology, the human's head is the center of their divine power and was given to them by Olodumare. The head is considered the most significant part of the human body. Hence, it is the home of the Ori. There are three different types of Ori. It mainly consists of the physical and spiritual aspects of a person.

## Ori Ode

The Ori Ode refers to the physical head. It isn't as significant as the Ori-inu. In fact, the value of the Ori-ode lies in its association with human beings and that it encompasses the spiritual head. Since the Ori-inu is invisible, the physical head symbolizes one's spiritual aspect and inner self.

## Ori-Inu

Ori-inu is the spiritual head that exists within the Ori-ode, and they can't be separated from one another. It represents the connection between the physical and spiritual aspects of a person. They are intertwined, and together, they represent one's identity.

The Ori or consciousness is the mysterious aspect of one personality, while the spiritual aspect is shrouded in mystery. This makes the Ori-inu a mystery existing inside another mystery. The Yoruba people describe the Ori-inu in an interesting way as the inner self that dances and moves *"in front of the mat."* Mat here represents the unity of all the divine's creation.

The Ori-inu is complex and rich. Even when a person reaches to unlock their Ori-ode, they will find a much more intricate layer that is mysterious and elusive. Interestingly, this is the source of their knowledge, yet it's still unknown to the Ori. In many Yoruba rituals and ceremonies, practitioners seek the help of the Orishas to uncover the secrets of the Ori-inu and reveal them to the Ori.

In the Yoruba faith, the newly initiated are prohibited from looking into mirrors because they can lose a part of themselves in the mirror and won't get it back until they can access the Ori-inu.

## Ori-Apere

The word Ori-Apere means patterns; in this case, it represents patterns of consciousness. In Yoruba mythology, energy patterns in every living being are referred to as "Odu." These patterns are repeated throughout creation. For instance, there are different types of fire, fire coming from an oven, the sun's fire, and fire from a match. They all share the same energy patterns but come from different sources. It's quite similar to the idea of reincarnation, where the spirit is reborn in different physical forms.

# FAQs

### Does everyone have an Ori?

Yes, everyone has an Ori. The concept of destiny has always been associated with mankind. Humanity would perish if one had nothing to look for or achieve. According to Yoruba mythology, each person must choose their own destiny.

### Can Ori be bad?

Yes and no. This question is open to many interpretations. No one chooses a bad destiny on purpose. However, some aspects can interfere with your Ori and make it bad. For instance, if the Orishas are angry, you'll experience many unfortunate events until you appease them. If you don't take advantage of the wisdom and knowledge of Ori, it will become bad. A bad character can also impact an Ori.

### Can I change my Ori?

Mythology varies here. Olodumare has the Oris of each person sealed and doesn't allow anyone to interfere with them. On the other hand, there are beliefs that you can improve your Ori and turn your luck around by connecting with your Ori and appeasing your Orisha. Ancient poems also tell of how Orunmila has changed the Ori of others. It is comforting to believe that one's destiny isn't fixed and can be changed,

### Do all people fulfill their Ori?

According to the Yoruba belief, each person must fulfill their Oris. However, if they fail, they can try again in another life when reincarnated.

### Can Olodumare or the Orishas alter my Ori or mess with it?

None of these beings can impact your Ori. A person's destiny is their choice, and no deity can change your chosen destiny, no matter how powerful. Only Orisha Orunmila has this power but will never interfere unless you invoke him.

### Is my Ori attached to me or separated?

An Ori is attached to you. It is similar to the concept of the aura, something that is always there, but you can't see it nor separate yourself from it.

### Will I discover my Ori?

Yes, but not right away. You will not discover your destiny as a whole. An Ori reveals itself little by little.

### Do we remember our Oris?

We forget our Oris the moment we come to Earth. Life would be dull if everyone became aware of their destiny.

### Does Ori mean that everything happens for a reason?

In Yoruba, there are no coincidences, and nothing is random. Everything is planned from the moment one chooses their Ori.

### How can I fulfill my Ori?

You can fulfill their Ori by achieving wisdom through integrating your heart and mind or emotions and thoughts.

In life, there are many mysteries and unanswered questions. Although mysterious, the concept of the Ori can answer some of life's biggest questions, like why are we here? Simply, to fulfill our Ori. It sheds light and explains many mysteries in life. People always ask "why" questions whenever they encounter unfortunate events like Why me? Why now? Some religions teach their followers not to ask these questions, as everything happens for a reason or a part of God's plan. This answer isn't always satisfactory, and one may need more information.

The concept of Ori explains that everything is part of a plan, but it is *your plan*. Everything that happens to you is mainly to help you fulfill the destiny you have chosen for yourself. You don't need to ask yourself why? Because all answers lie in the destiny you chose for yourself. The closer you get to fulfilling it, the clearer things will become and the fewer questions you'll have.

Nothing has more influence or a bigger impact on every aspect of one's life than their Ori. A person's main purpose in life is to fulfill their destiny. Every action you take moves you closer to your Ori. It gives you purpose even when you aren't aware of it. Human beings are on this Earth with one purpose only, to discover and fulfill their Oris.

Ori is a universal concept that exists in all religions, not just African-based practices. It just has a different name, but no matter what you believe in, no one can deny or escape their destiny.

The concept of the Ori is as complex as it is fascinating. The idea of destiny exists in all religions and faiths. However, Yoruba portrays it differently by giving all the power to human beings rather than to the deity. This raises the question, does one operate on free will or destiny? The next chapter will answer this universal question that people have been pondering for centuries.

# Chapter 3: Destiny vs. Free Will in Yoruba

In Yoruba, there is a long-standing debate between destiny and free will. This debate is deeply rooted in the traditional beliefs of the Yoruba people and has been echoed for centuries through their oral literature, religious practices, and philosophical traditions. On one side of this argument lies the belief that destiny or fate dictates the course of a person's life, and all outcomes are predetermined by a higher power. On the other side lies the belief that we have free will and that our actions directly influence our future. It is thought that within each of us waits a spark of divinity, which gives us the capability for free choice, no matter how small or insignificant it may be. Through examining the various perspectives of this debate, it is clear that Yoruba thought is far more nuanced and complex than what can be simplified into a binary choice. It exemplifies the complexities of human life as we continually search to make sense of our actions and place in the universe. Understanding both sides of this argument leads to an appreciation for all the possibilities our lives have to offer.

## Free Will in Yoruba

In Yoruba culture, the concept of free will is integral to daily life in many ways. A core belief is that each individual has autonomy and control over their own destiny and that they have the power to shape their circumstances. This idea is reflected through various traditional customs, such as offering sacrifices to the gods or wearing certain charms to influence outcomes. It's also often seen in the importance placed on dialogue and debate - talking things out instead of submitting to a predetermined outcome is at the center of many Yoruba cultures. These beliefs often extend beyond individuals, too, as collective action and working together for change are both seen as powerful ways to assert one's will or bring about an intended result. As conceived by Yoruba culture, free will is about much more than having choice or agency – it's about recognizing how every effort we make impacts our destiny, whether individually or collectively. Thus, it encourages individuals to strive toward the desired outcome using all available tools. Ultimately, free will in Yoruba culture serves as a reminder that you have the agency to live life on your terms. It emphasizes the understanding that no matter what external forces are at play, individuals will always have the power of choice when taking action toward reaching their goals. This positive outlook can be embraced by people from all walks of life.

## What Is Ori or Yoriba's Idea of Destiny?

In Yoruba culture, the concept of Ori is closely connected to destiny. At the time of a person's birth, it is believed that their Ori (or head) is joined with Olodumare, the supreme being of the universe. This connection allows people to access spiritual power, aligning them with their ultimate destiny. According to Yoruba tradition, this path must be followed during your life for you to fulfill your potential and achieve success. The Nollywood movie "Ori" (Head/Destiny), released in 1991–1992, addresses this idea uniquely and memorably. It follows three people struggling on various paths, trying to make sense of their fate and reach fulfillment and success. As they struggle through various challenges, they each come face-to-face with destiny as ordained by Olodumare – and ultimately reach a resolution. Much like in real life, it is only through embracing our Ori that we can take charge of our destiny and find our place in the world around us. As Yoruba philosopher Oduduwa once said: "If you want what you have never had, you'll have to do something you have never done before." It is up to us to listen to our Ori and step past fear or complacency, as only then will we be able to reach our full potential and achieve true success.

In the Yoruba people's belief system, Ori is a person's individual soul and inner being. It is seen as the part of oneself that determines destiny or the predetermined life path one should take. This idea stems from the idea that each person has a spiritual and physical guardian who helps guide them - called an Orisa - which is given at birth and remains with each individual for their entire life. Ori is believed to be connected to this Orisa and influences every aspect of your life in one way or another. The total of Ori's experiences determines an individual's future success, from health to wealth and even true love, making it a powerful force in dictating how life will play out for any given person. Believers strive to understand and align with their Ori to live prosperous lives. By meditating on the mystical connection between self and destiny, individuals can reach their highest potential while gaining clarity on their place in the world. According to traditional Yoruba beliefs, understanding your own Ori destiny is key to realizing fulfillment in life.

Beliefs surrounding Ori are vast and intertwined across many aspects of Yoruba culture and spirituality, giving rise to an important set of associated practices such as Ifa divination and maintaining spiritual order through ceremonial offerings for your Ori to remain balanced within. As a result, Ori has become firmly embedded as an integral part of history, tradition, ancestral reverence, moral righteousness, and personal identity within Yoruba culture – a testament perhaps to its important influence in revealing each individual's path toward thriving destiny outcomes in life. Whether you come from a place steeped in these traditions or have simply sought a greater understanding of Fate's influence over our life journey, grappling with Ori offers deep insights that may reveal your inner truth and connection with divinity more fully. Regardless of background or origin story, uncovering your Ori consciously helps orient you toward empowerment by revealing hidden gifts that help manifest personal growth milestones along life's spirit-led journey within intentions directed toward achieving freedom with grace!

# How Do the Different Components of Ori Work Together?

Yoruba is a powerful way to understand the world and our place in it. At its core, Yoruba revolves around the idea of destiny – or Ori. According to Yoruba tradition, this destiny is informed by four key components: Iwa (Inherent Character), Arugba (Divine Guidance), Ebo (Exchange), and Ori Inu (Head Situation). When considered together, these elements provide a comprehensive explanation for how our destinies are formed.

Iwa is a person's inherent character or spiritual make-up, which shapes who they are at their core. Arguably the most important piece of your destiny, Iwa includes physical traits such as eye color and deeper qualities like your ability to create meaningful relationships. This element also helps explain why people may be inclined to repeat certain behaviors despite trying different approaches.

Arugba is similar to divine grace and relates more closely to external influences that come with being part of a larger collective. It relates to benefits individuals receive from their community, family, and ancestors and serves as an appreciation for links to the past and future, emphasizing interconnection with others.

Ebo focuses on exchanges between people and the universe, particularly actions that either increase or alter an individual's luck or fortune to help further develop their destiny. Ebo can include offerings, prayers, and sacrifices made for something positive to happen. It is also closely related to reciprocity between people exchanging items or favors that ultimately facilitate growth in each other's lives.

Finally, Ori Inu represents the power of the head – literally, a person's physical head but also figuratively their mind or thinking – and aims to remind people that they have control over themselves through thoughts and beliefs. This control can range from simple decisions on how we lead our lives right up to controlling our connection with unseen forces. In all cases, it helps define and refine the personal definition of self beyond biological limits so true destiny can be achieved. When combined, these elements offer unlimited potential for growth which fuels an individual's pursuit of a truly meaningful life based on destiny as defined by Ori in Yoruba culture. By understanding these components, we can learn how different aspects fit together, allowing us to effectively embrace our destinies. This understanding offers us deep insight into ourselves, further aiding us along our life path while showing us the significance behind meanings placed in every aspect around us. Together, these elements offer unlimited potential for growth which fuels an individual's pursuit of meaning based on destiny as defined by Ori culture. By embracing this unique system of beliefs, we can learn how all parts work jointly together, allowing access to understand ourselves more fully and to find paths toward satisfying life's meaningful existence.

# How Can One Realign or Recreate Their Ori?

The concept of Ori or Head in Yoruba culture is deeply rooted in tradition and constantly evolving for each individual. It is a belief system that states that everyone carries their destiny within them - it works somewhat like a guiding force, balancing one's thoughts, emotions, and decisions. It cannot be created or changed entirely but can be aligned through rituals such as name-giving ceremonies, Ifa divination, and egungun masquerades. Generally speaking, changing one's Ori requires a consultation with an experienced Babalawo (diviner). This can help to realign your Ori if it has been disrupted by life events such as illness or a death in the family, and thus bring balance back into your life. As this consultative process unfolds, certain aspects of the Ori cannot be changed, no matter what. These sections are thought to represent parts of our collective identity, derived from our ancestry and handed down through generations of oral storytelling. However, many experts agree that you have control over those aspects of your Ori which relate to self-determination. This includes taking responsibility for decisions that impact the course of your life, including where or how you live, how you interact with people, what career paths you choose, and how you practice spirituality, etc. In essence, a person's Ori must be acknowledged as an integral part of their identity but also understood as something which can be affected by personal choices and decisions. Consequently, it becomes possible to adapt and modify one's journey over time without completely disregarding the foundations imposed by tradition or customs. At its core, the notion of an ancestral head serves as a constant reminder to reflect on the strength found in both dynamic change and deep-rooted acceptance within Yoruba culture.

To truly understand our Ori is to recognize the importance placed on honoring African heritage while recognizing our capacity for growth. Only then can individuals truly harness their ability to cultivate insight surrounding their destiny. According to Yoruba beliefs, when we live true to our authentic selves, we become spiritually connected with ourselves, family/community/ancestral bloodlines, etc., as well as with nature which surrounds us, ultimately understanding our Creator better to realize man's ultimate purpose on Earth is achieving peace and unity through love.

# Ori-Apere and How It Can Change an Individual's Ori

In Yoruba culture, Ori-Apere is used to help a person achieve balance and harmony within themselves. It refers to the "personal force" or spiritual power that an individual has, which influences their behavior and their life trajectory. Ori-Apere acts as a compass, helping guide the individual through physical and emotional challenges. In traditional Yoruba beliefs, when someone's Ori-Apere becomes out of balance due to adversity or great life changes, it needs to be restored for them to reach their full potential. This can be achieved through prayer, meditation, and other forms of spiritual practice. The aim is to reawaken the power of one's original self and reconnect with their higher purpose. Ultimately, if individuals can realign their Ori-Apere, they will have access to new energy, which will help them move forward in their journey while staying true to who they are. By taking the time and effort to restore their force, they will become better equipped for life's challenges, whatever form they may take. Ultimately this helps a person tap into new sources of inner strength, and it acts as a pointer enabling them to move ahead while continuing to be true to themselves. That gives them strength regardless of the type of adversities they encounter on their path toward greatness. After all, personal alignment is key for individuals who want to realize their full potential. Consequently, imbalances between physical, emotional, and mental states will greatly decrease, which could stop you from reaching your goals.

# Components of Ori-Apere

## 1. Ayanmo

Ayanmo is an integral component of Ori-Apere. It is one of the most important parts of Yoruba culture, which is closely associated with spiritual growth and personal harmony. Literally translated, Ayanmo means "*taking back the essence*" and refers to the process of getting back in touch with the divine source and restoring balance in both body and mind. This concept is based on the belief that every person has three souls. These are the physical (which resides in the body), the astral (which exists within and beyond space), and the spiritual (which is connected to a higher power).

Through meditation and introspection, an individual can develop their connection with these three souls, aligning themselves with their higher purpose. Taking part in these activities helps individuals understand what motivates them and guides them toward achieving greater self-awareness. By bringing balance to an individual's spiritual life, Ayanmo helps people live more harmoniously with themselves and their loved ones while fostering an unshakeable faith in divine order. Furthermore, it reaffirms that each person needs to be mindful of expressions from all three planes: physical, astral, and spiritual – for total fulfillment and enlightenment. Ayanmo is truly a foundational element for any who seeks deeper meaning in life or wishes to unlock greater inner potential in accordance with traditional Yoruba culture.

## 2. Akunleya

Found mainly in Nigeria, Akunleya is an important component of Yoruba culture. It is the concept of using respectful speech at all times, regardless of who we are speaking to and the situation; essentially, it refers to etiquette in conversation. Akunleya means politeness and refraining from talking about uncomfortable or controversial topics. This concept is based on respect for others as well as for ourselves. It plays an essential role in many aspects of life, from familial and communal relationships to business dealings. Proper use of Akunleya encourages a peaceful social environment. It allows people to problem-solve instead of clashing with one another.

Moreover, it fosters trust between individuals, helping them to build beneficial relationships based on mutual understanding and respect. Akunleya is part of Ori-Apere, which translates roughly to *"personal character"* or the practices a person should uphold if he wishes to be respected by his peers. The principle of Akunleya runs deep within the fabric of Yoruba culture, encouraging people toward empathetic conversations rather than heated disagreements. It serves as a reminder that polite speech should always be prioritized when interacting with one another.

## 3. Akunlegba

Akunlegba is more than just semantics; it carries a deep meaning for the Yoruba. In essence, this concept speaks to the physical, spiritual, and intellectual transformation that must take place in order for a person to be well-rounded. Physically, Akunlegba holds that we must work actively to develop and maintain a healthy lifestyle that can sustain life over time.

Those who adhere to these ideals seek physical strength and mental agility. Spiritually, Akunlegba emphasizes living a life with a mindset of understanding and respect for faith, taking responsibility for personal development, and outwardly practicing virtuous behavior through service to others. Intellectually, Akunlegba encourages individuals to hone their comprehension by engaging in analysis, critical thinking, and knowledgeable communication across cultures – basically mental transnationalism or education beyond one's individual faith system or culture. In summation, Akunlegba is a philosophical requirement essential to developing an authentic understanding of ourselves and our environment in the Yoruba context – both the tangible and the intangible aspects – serving as a guidepost for proper socialization throughout each person's life journey. By adhering to tenants like these within Ori-Apere, individuals holistically evolve into wise stewards who protect natural assets through sustainable practices while inspiring others to do the same.

Akunlegba is viewed as a gateway between heaven and earth, acting as a mediator between both realms. It involves rituals designed to open a connection between gods and spirits on the one hand and humans on the other. According to legend, man is said to descend from God through such gateways, encoded in various objects purchased by practitioners for use during spiritual cleansing or invocation ceremonies at altars. Those who partake in such festivities often receive guidance from godly energy forces or divinities that intermingle within these points of contact between heaven and Earth. Furthermore, it is also believed that utilizing Akunlegba's energies and aligning with divine powers through ancestral worship can reveal solutions to deal with unfavorable states and circumstances, keeping those relying on traditional methods of divination from achieving success and gaining purpose within life's journey toward destiny. Therefore, anyone seeking self-development or healing can explore this age-old practice as an effective solution to present predicaments. In conclusion, by utilizing this powerful component found within Ori-Apere, practitioners can utilize its wisdom, harnessed ages ago, to alter the destinies of individuals today to bring forth blessings and harmony in the mortal plain.

In conclusion, the debate between destiny and free will in Yoruba thought is a complex one that has been argued for centuries. It reflects the complexities of human life and encourages us to consider our actions carefully and make the choices that suit us best. It is up to each person to decide which side of the debate they believe in and how they will shape the course of their destiny. By understanding both sides of this argument, we can gain an appreciation for all that life has to offer.

# Chapter 4: Olodumare and the Orishas

Aside from being described as a way of explaining someone's destiny and purpose, Ori is also often described as Olodumare's spark inside a person. It is a gift to humans and, therefore, can be understood better by understanding Olodumare and the Orishas.

This chapter will help you understand the importance of Olodumare to the Yoruba religion, explore the creation story in depth, and go over the concept of the Orishas. At the end of this chapter, you'll have a better understanding of Yoruba cosmology, and you'll be better able to understand the role of Ori in it.

## Understanding Olodumare

Olodumare is one of the many names for the Yoruba supreme deity. Other names include Olorun and Olafin-Orun. Olodumare is the traditional name given to this supreme deity in the Yoruba language. The name "Olorun" has gained popularity due to the influence of other religions on Isese, including Christianity and Islam.

Olodumare is depicted in many ways in different cultures.
*https://commons.wikimedia.org/wiki/File:Tutelary_Deity_or_Guardian_Figure_(alusi),_Nigeria,_Igbo_people,_c._1935,_wood,_paint_-_Chazen_Museum_of_Art_-_DSC01780.JPG*

Olodumare is not only a sky and creator god; this deity is considered to be the "owner of life." In Yoruba, Olodumare is completely unique, and no other deity can come close. This uniqueness is reflected in the fact that, in the Yoruba language, Olodumare has no gender. Olodumare is purely a spiritual entity, unlike the Orishas.

As the owner of life, Olodumare is immortal, omnipotent, and omniscient. However, Olodumare is also aloof from humanity and communicates with the world through their helpers, the Orishas. For this reason, there is no image or shrine of Olodumare, nor are any sacrifices made directly to the creator deity. Very few Yoruba people worship Olodumare directly. Instead, they worship them through the agency and actions of the Orishas.

Olodumare is called to primarily when prayers to the other Orishas seem to go unanswered. This deity is not only immortal, omniscient, and omnipotent – they are also all-knowing and good and evil. Olodumare is, essentially, a representation of all the aspects of the universe.

The many names given to Olodumare reflect this deity's multiple roles as the head of the Yoruba pantheon. These names include:

- **Olofi:** The ruler of the Earth and the conduit between Orun (heaven) and Aye (Earth)
- **Olodumare:** The creator deity
- **Olorun:** The ruler of the heavens
- **Alaaye:** The living/everlasting one
- **Elemi:** The keeper/owner of life. As the keeper of life, Olodumare bestows "life breath" upon humans. When Olodumare withdraws this life breath, the person dies.
- **Olojo Oni:** Owner/controller of the day and daily happenings. This name implies that a person's destiny (Ori) is in the hands of Olodumare and their plan for humanity.

Because Olodumare is primarily distant from humanity, much of the connection between them and humanity is fostered by the creator's emissaries or helpers, the Orishas. The Yoruba creation myth is one of the most important stories to reflect this relationship.

# The Yoruba Creation Myth

According to the Yoruba creation myth, in the beginning, the world consisted of nothing but the sky, the water, and the wild marshlands. Olodumare and the Orishas lived in the sky, above a young baobab tree, and descended and ascended to and from the marshlands below using a chain (or, in some versions of the story, a spider's web). During this time, there were no humans because there was no land for them to live on.

However, the Orisha Obatala was unsatisfied and, unlike the other Orishas, was not content to stay near the baobab tree and Olodumare. Instead, he was curious and would often look at the waters and wild marshlands below the sky. One day, when he was looking into the waters, he decided that the world needed more than that.

So, he traveled to Olodumare and asked the creator deity for permission to create solid land in the waters below. There, the Orishas and Olodumare could create beings who the Orishas could aid using their powers. Because of this, in one version of the story, Obatala is referred to as the Head of the White Cloth (that is, the Head of the fabric of creation).

Olodumare agreed to this request from Obatala. Having gained the permission he was seeking, Obatala then went to Orunmila, the Orisha of wisdom and divination, and asked him how he should prepare for his journey to the world below.

By reading the patterns of palm kernels and the powder of baobab roots, Orunmila told Obatala that he must create a chain of gold that he could use to travel to the world below. He would also have to gather sand, palm nuts, maize, plant seeds, a white hen, and have a black cat with him. Finally, he would have to carry the sacred egg, which contained the Orishas' personalities.

After hearing this, Obatala traveled from Orisha to Orisha, asking them to donate their gold. When he gathered gold from every Orisha, he had the goldsmith use it to create a chain. He also gathered all the sand in the sky and placed it in a snail shell, which he would use to carry it down to the waters with him. In the snail shell, he sprinkled some baobab powder. He gathered everything he needed, placed it in his pack, and carried the sacred egg close to his chest.

Once he had everything he needed, he hooked the golden chain to the sky and began climbing down to the waters below. For seven days, he traveled downwards until he reached the waters below.

When he reached the waters, he hung from the end of the chain and was confused, unsure of what he should do to create land. Seeing his confusion, Orunmila called to him, telling him to use the sand he had collected. He poured the sand into the waters and dropped the hen with it. The hen pecked at the sand, spreading it around, where it solidified and turned into land.

While Obatala was hanging from the end of the chain, his heart was pounding so much that it cracked the egg he was carrying close to his chest. From it emerged Sankofa, the sacred bird that carried the spirits of the Orishas. As Sankofa began to fly, it stirred up the sand and created a storm, blowing the sand here and there. This created hills, lowlands, dunes, and mountains, giving the land a unique character, just like each Orisha had a unique character.

Finally, Obatala let go of the chain, dropping onto the newly created land. He named this land "Ife," the place/land that divides the waters. Curious about this new land, he started walking around and exploring. As he walked, he planted the palm nuts he had carried with him, which sprouted into palm trees. He also scattered the other seeds he had in his pack, turning the barren land green with trees and plants.

The black cat he had carried from the heavens, Obatala, kept him company. However, he soon began to grow lonely – and thirsty. In his thirst, he stopped at the edge of a pond. However, before he could quench his thirst, his attention was grabbed by his own reflection in the pond. Seeing it, Obatala was pleased and decided to create beings like him to keep him company.

Using the dark earth clay at the pond's edge, Obatala began his task of forming these beings. However, he soon grew tired and even thirstier. He used juice from his newly planted palm trees to ferment into palm wine to satisfy his thirst. However, he soon grew intoxicated, and in his intoxication, he continued to create the clay figures.

However, unlike his initial figures, these figures were not perfect. Instead, they were misshapen, some without eyes, or with misshapen limbs, or many other imperfections. However, Obatala thought that these figures were beautiful, so he continued to create them.

While he was creating these figures, Olodumare sent down the Chameleon to check on Obatala's progress. The Chameleon reported back that Obatala had created figures with proper form but that he was disappointed in their lack of life.

In response, Olodumare gathered the gasses of the universe beyond the sky and sparked them into a fireball. He sent this fireball to Ife, where it dried the still-wet figures and baked them. The fireball also caused the earth to start spinning. Then, Olodumare blew across Ife, bestowing the figures with the gift of life and giving birth to the first people of Ife – and the first humans.

The next day, Obatala came to his senses and realized that, in his intoxication, he had brought deformity to the world. Regretting his actions, he vowed never to drink again and took the role of the protector of those born deformed.

Obatala's new people started to build huts and soon formed the first Yoruba village. Obatala returned to the heavens but split his time between Ife and the sky.

All the other Orishas were pleased with Obatala's work except Olokun. Olokun was the Orisha of the bottom of the ocean, and, as such, the waters below the world were part of her domain. Ife was created without her permission, and Obatala usurped much of her kingdom through his creation.

In her wrath, Olokun sent wave after wave from her oceans to destroy Obatala's creation and succeeded in destroying much of the kingdom. Obatala, who was visiting the sky at the time, was unaware of this until the survivors in Ife sent a message with Esu, the messenger Orisha, to Olodumare and Obatala, asking for help.

Upon hearing the news, Obatala climbed down to the Earth, which caused the waters to recede, ending the great flood. Worried that Olokun would cause another flood when he returned to the heavens, he challenged her to a weaving contest and sent Chameleon to Olokun to judge her skill. As Olokun wove, Chameleon changed color to mimic the fabric. Realizing that she couldn't beat Chameleon, Olokun accepted her defeat and agreed to stop her wrath. Thus, the people of Ife were free to live and reproduce.

It should be noted that this is only the best-known version of the Yoruba creation myth. In a variation of the myth, Obatala was not the Orisha who devised the idea of creating the land and humanity. Instead, it was the idea of Olodumare, and it was Olodumare who told Obatala to fulfill this mission. In this version of the story, every action that Obatala took was dictated by Olodumare and not Orunmila.

That said, regardless of the version, what is clear is that Olodumare remained one step removed from humanity. It was not the creator god who actually created humanity. It was Obatala who formed clay into the first humans. Olodumare was the deity who gave humanity life. Because of this, Olodumare is now worshiped as the aloof creator deity, while Obatala is venerated as the creator of humanity and the founder and first king of Ife.

# The Orishas

Given that Olodumare is primarily aloof from humanity, their guidance must be carried out by their emissaries, the Orishas.

The Orishas are essentially the gods or deities of Yoruba belief. They are emanations/avatars of Olodumare, created to bring Olodumare's guidance to the universe. There are hundreds, even thousands of Orishas, and it is most often described that there are "400 + 1" Orishas in the Yoruba pantheon: a way of saying that the Orishas are innumerable.

That said, while there are "400+1" Orishas, some are more prominent than others. It is primarily 20 or 30 Orishas who appear in the stories of the Yoruba pantheon. Of them, 7 are more prominent than the others: Esu, Ogun, Obatala, Yemaya, Oshun, Shango, and Oya.

The Orishas are meant to help humans achieve their Ori and self-actualize. However, they are not meant to be perfect deities and have their own personality and flaws. Because of this, they can occasionally get in the way of people achieving their Ori, whether purposefully or unknowingly. An Orisha may purposefully take steps to prevent a person from self-actualizing because the person has offended the Orisha and therefore has brought punishment upon themselves.

Seeing how Orishas are capable of weakness, pride, desire, spite, and arrogance, their relationship with Olodumare is complex and often hard to understand. In one well-known story, the Orishas tire of Olodumare's aloofness from humanity and the Orishas, and they plot to overthrow Olodumare as the supreme deity.

However, the Orishas forgot to include Esu in their plan. They plotted to scare Olodumare to death by inviting them to a hut and releasing mice inside, which the creator deity was terrified of. Esu, who was present in the doorway when the plot was being hatched, heard everything.

On the agreed-upon day, Olodumare arrived at the hut where the mice were hidden and crossed the threshold when the door was closed, and the mice were released. Olodumare was terrified and tried to run but could not. The door was closed. However, Esu appeared and ate the mice. He then pointed out the guilty Orishas to Olodumare, who punished them and rewarded Esu.

In another story, the Orishas once again attempted to overthrow Olodumare. After knowing their plan, Esu arrived at Olodumare's realm and let them know. In return, Olodumare stopped the rains from falling to the Earth. As a result, the waters of the Earth dried up, crops began to fail, and the Orishas repented their actions. However, the Orishas couldn't reach the palace of Olodumare to plead their case.

Finally, Oshun turned herself into a peacock and flew to Olodumare's palace. She lost most of her feathers during the journey and arrived exhausted and ill, having turned into a vulture. Taking pity on her state, Olodumare finally heard the Orishas' pleas and allowed the rains to fall on the Earth again. As a reward for her actions, Olodumare named Oshun the messenger of heaven, the only one who was granted leave to bring messages to Olodumare's palace.

Thus, though the Orishas are emanations and emissaries of Olodumare, they are not always aligned. However, in most cases, the Orishas attend to their duties, acting as the go-betweens between humanity and Olodumare. While every Orisha has a role to play, the seven most prominent Orishas are the ones who are best-known and most worshiped. These seven Orishas are most commonly referred to as gods and goddesses.

### Esu

Trickster deities are common in many African belief systems, and Isese is no different. In the Yoruba religion, Esu serves as the trickster deity. However, he was not only a mischief-maker – but he was also the Orisha who brought balance to the world.

Esu is the Orisha of duality, balance, crossroads, beginnings, and orderliness. He was also the *messenger Orisha*, the one who ruled over travelers, chaos, death, and misfortune. He was a complex, dual-natured Orisha who now teaches believers that there are two or more sides to every issue and is also known as "A-bá-ni-wá-òràn-bá-ò-rí-dá" (He-who-creates-problems-for-the-innocent).

Even though he is an unpredictable Orisha, he is also necessary for order in life. Because of his importance, he is the only Orisha to be worshiped every day of the traditional four-day Yoruba week.

### Ogun

Ogun is the Orisha of blacksmiths, craftsmen, metalworkers, iron, soldiers, and war. He is the owner of all technology, and as a warrior deity, all technology shares in his nature, and it is used first and foremost for war.

It is said that using his metal ax, Ogun clears the way for the other Orishas to enter the Earth. In the Yoruba creation myth, the gold chain that Obatala used to reach the waters is symbolic of Ogun and his role in clearing the way for the other Orishas.

It is said that Ogun was the first king of Ife as a human. After his death, he disappeared into the earth in the town of Ire-Ekiti, vowing to help those who called on him. The symbols of Ogun are the dog, the palm frond, and iron. He is often depicted with a spitting cobra and is recognized with the number seven and the colors black and green.

### Obatala

Obatala is the sky father, the eldest of Olodumare's Orishas. He is the Orisha of creation, the sky, light, and morality.

In some stories, Obatala was also the founder and the first king of Ife-Ife. After his death, he was deified and merged with the Orisha Obatala.

He had 201 wives, with his principal wife being Yemaya. However, in some stories, his favorite wife was Yemowo. He is associated with the color white. White contains all the colors of the rainbow and therefore shows that Obatala opens different paths. Additionally, Obatala is the Head of the White Cloth. Thus, white is associated with him.

### Yemaya

Also known as Yemoja, Yemaya was the Mother of All Water. She was the mother of all Orishas and was the Orisha of creation, water, motherhood, pregnant women, and all the waters on the Earth. She was also made the patron Orisha of the Ogun River.

She is often portrayed as a mermaid or dressed in seven skirts of blue and white. One of Yemaya's names means "Mother Whose Children are Fish," and she is mother to uncountable children – as many there are fish in the ocean. Yemaya is a gentle, caring Orisha who is slow to anger, but her wrath is destructive and violent when she is angered.

### Oshun

Oshun is the Orisha of the sweet waters of the world and is also the Orisha of love, beauty, intimacy, diplomacy, and wealth. She is the patron deity of the Osun River and is honored during the two-week-long annual Osun-Osogbo festival that takes place in the city of Osogbo.

In one version of the Yoruba creation myth, it is said that Oshun, along with 16 other Orishas, was sent to create the world. Oshun was the youngest and only female, Orisha, and so she was ignored by the others. When the 16 male Orishas failed to create the world, they turned to Olodumare for help. Olodumare told them that creation could not happen without Oshun's help, so they returned and apologized to her. She accepted their apology and finished creating the world, bringing beauty, fertility, love, and sweetness to it.

While this is a less popular version of the Yoruba creation myth, it demonstrates the importance of Oshun in the Yoruba pantheon.

It is said that she was once mortal and, during her mortal life, attended a drum festival and fell in love with Shango, who made her his second wife. Despite not being his chief wife, she is his favorite. She is associated with the colors gold and yellow and the number five. In the traditional Yoruba creation myth, she is represented by the white hen, which was said to have five fingers.

### Shango

Perhaps the most "popular" Orisha among worshippers, Shango is also the strongest Orisha in the Yoruba pantheon. He is the Orisha of lightning and thunder, fire, justice, dance, and virility, and is similar to storm gods in other pantheons.

A hot-blooded, strong-willed Orisha, he took the form of the third Alaafin of Oyo for a short period of time. In his time as mortal ruler, he was violent and bloodthirsty – but also one of the most powerful Yoruba rulers.

Shango was the husband of three wives – Oba, Oshun, and Oya. Of these, Oshun was his favorite. He is worshiped on the fifth day of the week, and foods consumed as part of his worship include bitter kola, guguru, amala, and gbegiri soup. He is associated with the color red and the numbers four and six and is represented by his powerful double-headed ax.

### Oya

Oya is the third and youngest wife of Shango. She is the Orisha of storms, thunder and lightning, and the wind. She is also the guardian of the dead and the deity of transformation. She is also known as Oya-Ìyáńsàn-án (the mother of nine). This refers to the nine children she birthed, all of whom were stillborn.

She is the patron deity of the river Niger and is a warrior Orisha. It is said that she rides into war at the side of Shango and that she is unbeatable in battle. As a deity of change, she commands the essence of the constantly changing world around us and is the ruler of gifts like intuition and clairvoyance.

# Chapter 5: Ori as an Orisha

By reading this chapter, you'll find out all about the different methods you can use to worship your Ori. You'll understand how to reach out to it as a single powerful entity and as an Orisha. Then, you'll find the basics of worshiping an Orisha.

## Worshiping Ori

According to Yoruba, we all possess physical and spiritual self-healing powers that we can unlock by connecting with and worshiping the Orishas. Over time, this type of work can help us become more balanced, which allows us to align with our higher selves (Ori). Some practitioners suggest that one's Ori can be worshiped as an Orisha. After all, you can reach out to your divine self for guidance whenever you encounter a problem. You should also appease your Ori whenever things go wrong. Yoruba suggests that everything happening in your life is overseen by your Ori. Ori can be thought of as a spirit with an immense amount of power that lies between humans and God.

Everyone connects with their Ori in a unique way. Some people like to take simple approaches, while others believe that an Ori should be appeased like an Orisha. You can simply praise your Ori in the morning, express your love and appreciation toward it, and ask it for guidance or abundance. You can achieve an aligned and secure sense of self by regularly reaching out to your Ori. You'll eventually find yourself being naturally guided as if this sense of direction is coming from within. Others find it beneficial to have deep conversations with their Ori.

Those who prefer a more complete approach typically prefer rituals. While some rituals must be conducted by Orisha priests, there are others that you can try out if you believe you're qualified enough to do so. If you decide to do it yourself, you should ask an experienced practitioner to supervise the process until you get the hang of it.

# Connecting with Your Ori

You have to explore your Ori and understand what it is to ensure that you're connecting with your Ori in the right way. If you don't have a background in astrology, you'll need to seek the guidance of a professional astrologer. You'll need to know more about what your birthdate entails, the areas in your life in which you're most aligned and abundant, and the aspects in which you're not.

To start connecting with your Ori, you must be living life in a way that's true to who you are. You'll never be able to align with your Ori if you don't embrace your true, authentic nature. The key is to be completely honest, not only with yourself but with others too.

If you wish to align with your Ori, you need to spend time with people you feel great around. Don't force yourself to fit into a social circle that has different values and beliefs you don't agree with, especially if you have to hide your own convictions and pretend to be someone you're not around them. Surrounding yourself with like-minded individuals encourages you to express yourself and feel at ease. It also makes it a lot easier for you to stay focused on things that matter and not lose sight of your goals.

Regularly surrounding yourself with nature can help you align with your divine self because it keeps you grounded, which can allow you to truly connect with your inner self. Spending time in nature is a great way to clear your mind and soothe your anxiety. Shutting down your intrusive and unnecessary thoughts allows you to pay more attention to your feelings, emotions, and true thoughts. Some practitioners believe that God manifests himself as the supreme deity through nature, which means that regularly spending time in nature can enrich your spiritual endeavors.

Surround yourself with nature to stay grounded and connect with the divine.
https://www.pexels.com/photo/photography-of-a-woman-meditating-906097/

Meditation is another great way to strengthen your connection with your Ori. One mantra that you can chant repetitively is the "Haaaaa." Take a deep breath and exhale while saying the mantra. You can also chant "O Ree Mo Pay Oh" three times, followed by "Or ree Sahn me" and "Or ree Sahn Ee get ee." Reciting this chant allows you to call to your divine self for guidance and support. Keep in mind that you may need to experiment with different techniques and chants until you find one that works for your Ori.

Exercising or doing Yoga can help you connect with your Ori because physical activities encourage your body to release the tension it's been storing. When you're exercising, pay attention to your breathing pattern. Yoga is great at helping you connect with your Ori because it teaches you to control and connect with your breath. This is why this mindfulness practice can help you regulate your thoughts and feelings, which leads to the overall peace of mind.

# Ibori: Feed Your Ori

If you wish to take the other approach, you can conduct a very powerful yet relatively easy ritual. The Ori cleansing and feeding practices are known as Ibori. Remember that the following version of the ritual is the most basic. There's another much more complex practice. It must be conducted by an Orisha priest or an experienced Babalawo; hence the practice explained below will help you as a beginner.

To conduct this ritual, you must have some background in divinatory practices as you'll be determining when and if you need to perform an Ibori and which offerings you need to give to your divine self. You must also learn to tell whether your higher self has accepted your offering and if they're appeased. You'll benefit from using Opèle or Ikin and knowing the positions of the Odu IFA, as they can offer clear and distinct answers. Make sure you consult an Orisha priest to help you consecrate your IFA divination tools beforehand.

# Choosing Your Offerings

Offerings can include many options.
https://pxhere.com/en/photo/1363848

Cast IFA to determine if your Ori currently needs to receive an offering and which offerings it wants. If you can't determine what to give to your Ori via divinatory practices, you can try a few of the following offerings:

- Meat is used to generate strength.

- Fruit attracts abundance and revitalizes your destiny

- Omiero is typically used in various rituals

- Dry gin can attract pleasure and resilience

- Native chalk is a popular ritual offering

- Honey can bring joy into one's life

- Shea butter is used for protection and calm

- Cool water is refreshing and soothing
- Coconut milk is known for being a cooling and calming agent
- Red palm oil is great for attracting abundance, ease, and sustenance
- Kola-nut is invigorating and vivacious. It can help you steer clear of challenges and roadkill and is good for fostering wisdom.
- Sugar cane can bring an element of agreeableness and pleasance into your life
- Bitter Kola is used to attract longevity and protection.

# Preparing Omiero

While it's best if you ask a professional Babalawo to prepare Omiero for you, you can still do it yourself if you don't have access to an Orisha priest. Oftentimes, the liquid is made from water and a blend of specific herbs. Some Yorubas incorporate snail blood or blood from other animals into the solution. Omiero is believed to be Obatala's most preferred offering.

Omiero is used to wash one's head, the Ori, because it can attract good fortune, tranquility, and peace of mind. It also allows you to nourish your head with some elements of Orunmila and Obatala throughout the practice.

The best Omiero ingredients for Ibori are ewe ero, white native chalk, coconut water, shea butter, spring water, soft meat, and snail blood. You can add any amount of each ingredient to the blend but try to follow your intuition as you do so. You should be particular and clear about your intentions as you add each ingredient. Name the reason why you're adding each ingredient to the Omiero. When you've finished, you can bathe in it.

Note that you should be very careful about what you put on your Ori because it's really sensitive. While this blend is popularly used during Ibori rituals, each person's Ori requires unique offerings and responds differently. This is why you should determine which ingredients to use via divinatory practices or by consulting a Babalawo.

# Getting Ready

You should try performing Ibori in the morning before interacting with anyone. However, many people don't like to do that because performing Ibori requires you to stay at home for the rest of the day. If this isn't practical for you, you can perform the ritual in the evening when you're sure that you won't have to go out for the rest of the day. Your home – or at least room – should be free of disturbances during the entire ritual. Steer clear of anything that may hinder your peace of mind.

Take a bath or shower, and use consecrated black soap to wash your head before you present your offering. This allows you to wash away any negative energy you may have gathered. When you're in the shower, you should imagine that your spiritual, mental, and emotional dirt is being washed away. You can spend as much time as you want as long as you come out of the shower feeling relaxed and clean (physically, emotionally, mentally, and spiritually). Get dressed in all-white (or the next lightest color you have) clothes and undergarments. Avoid dark and bright clothes.

If you have an Igba'Ori, you should use it to perform your ritual. You can also perform your ceremony at an ancestral shrine if you have one set up. If not, choose a quiet and comfortable space to begin. The room should be clean, organized, and consecrated with Holy water. Conducting your preferred form of divination can also help you get rid of negative energy before you start the ritual.

# Performing Ibori

1. Throw the cool water and earth around and call each of their names out. Call on the ancestors and Orunmila.
2. Use palm oil, kola, or power to anoint your tongue.
3. The tongue carries "ofo ase," which means the power of words. This is why you should say that the ase of the deities, or Orisha, is in your mouth as you do so.
4. Pay homage by chanting Iba and Oriki
5. Offer your chosen sacrifices to feed your Ori.

Start at the position of your third eye and move to the top of your head and down to the base of your skull. Do that with each offering and mention the reason why you're feeding your Ori this particular item. For example, you can say something like, *"Ori, please give me strength as I give you meat for resilience."*

Creamy and liquid offerings should be dabbed with the liquid middle finger and smudged between your eyes, around your eyebrows, and moving upward and down the base of your skull. Solid items should be presented to the forehead. Use the same finger to present your offerings to your navel and your index finger to present them to your right toe.

Secure all the offerings you've placed on your head using a special white cloth. You should keep wearing the white headscarf with the offerings underneath for the rest of the day, even after you've finished your ceremony. It helps deflect unwanted energies.

6. Cast IFA to determine whether your Ori has accepted your offerings.

7. Pay your homage by chanting Iba.

## Closing the Ibori Ritual

Use Opèle or Ikin to determine whether your Ori wants another offering. In some cases, one's Ori may request an additional item in particular or ask you to repeat a certain chant or prayer. You shouldn't close your ceremony if you're not sure that your Ori is satisfied or has accepted all your offerings.

Try to maintain your peace of mind, avoid doing a lot of physical or mental work, and refrain from sexual activities for the rest of the day. Remove your offerings the following morning before you shower. Make sure you ask your Ori where they would like you to discard the items.

## Worshiping the Orishas

You don't need to perform daily rituals in order to worship the Orishas. However, you should regularly recite your personal prayers and offer the appropriate sacrifices. The prayers and sacrifices you choose mainly depend on your divinatory revelations, your intuition, and the preferences of the Orisha that you're worshiping. Many people opt for fruit offerings, as they're generally favored among the deities and are associated with abundance.

Yorubas engage in communal celebrations during which they conduct drumming and dancing ceremonies as a form of prayer. These celebrations can also help induce a trance or altered state of consciousness, which can help practitioners connect with the spiritual world more effectively.

Each Orisha requires different objects to be placed on their altars. While some deities may prefer certain offerings, others may not accept them. This is why you should be very mindful about what you place on your shrine. Here are some examples of what you can place on the altars of a few Orishas:

## Obatala

- Metal crown
- Bell with a dove-shaped handle
- White cloth (opt for a cotton material)
- White candle
- Statue or picture of Obatala
- Rice, cocoa butter, meringue, eggs, or other white offerings. Your offerings should be bland and not overwhelmingly flavorful. Avoid spicy foods, salt, and alcohol.

## Shango

- Axe
- Sword
- Crown
- Wooden bowl with a cover
- Pedestal
- Wooden tools
- Drum
- Statue or picture of Shango
- Red or white candle
- Opt for spicy, red, and hot offerings

## Yemaya

- Shells (preferably cowrie)
- Silver items
- Statues or pictures of dolphins, mermaids, fish, or other sea creatures

- Pearls
- Fans
- Blue or white candle
- Blue cloth
- Incense
- Blue or colorful lowers
- Your offerings should include seafood, fruits, lettuce, white wine, and coffee

Now that you have read this chapter, you understand how to worship your Ori as either a single powerful spirit or as an Orisha. You also understand the basics of worshiping Yoruba Orishas and know how to choose your offerings for both your Ori and the deity you're worshiping. If you wish to cultivate a strong connection with the Orishas, you must always start by aligning with your Ori.

# Chapter 6: You and Your Ancestors

Ancestors are spiritual entities who can significantly influence your life in alignment with your Ori. After reading this chapter, you'll learn everything you need to know about the concept and importance of "Egungun." You'll also understand the types and levels of Yoruba ancestors and learn the basics of working with them. Finally, you'll find out how to reach out to your ancestors.

## The Idea of Life and Death

Working with your ancestors is one of the best ways to overcome any challenges you face in life. They can provide you with the needed guidance and support. According to Yorubas, a person's connection with their ancestors must be held in the highest regard. It is considered a very intimate bond. Practitioners bury their loved ones at home instead of in the cemetery so they can wish them good morning and good night and share with them their joy and pain. Yoruba beliefs don't think of death as the end of existence, nor does it view death as a separation between those who are alive and those who have passed on. Yorubas simply think of death as a mode of transportation from one realm or state of existence to the other.

Yorubas use the word "Ódàbọ̀" when communicating with their loved ancestors. This means that the person is looking forward to reuniting with their ancestor, whether literally, spiritually, via visualization practices, or in their dreams. Practitioners believe that they can reunite with their ancestors by worshiping them or allowing themselves to feel all the emotions and experience the necessary realizations associated with losing a loved one.

Yorubas think of death as a beginning and not an end. It doesn't suggest that something has ended. Instead, it indicates that new possibilities are coming to life. In Yoruba, a male ancestor is known as Egún (Egúngún is the plural form), and a female ancestor is known as Gèlèdè. When practicing Yoruba, you must make peace with the idea of death. Otherwise, you'll never feel free and will think of death as something to be feared. It is then viewed as a danger that should be avoided instead of a passage to a new world. While Yorubas do grieve when they lose a loved one, they view death as a celebration for the most part. This view of life and death allows them to accept reality and the cycle of being.

## Types and Levels of Yoruba Ancestors

Yorubas believe that there are two types of death. One is socially accepted, and the other isn't. The former refers to deaths occurring at a late stage in life, while the latter refers to deaths occurring earlier and unexpectedly. People who die young are called "Àbíkú," which is a term associated with premature death. Àbíkú is thought to be born only to die young. Yorubas believe that worshiping and working closely with their ancestors can help them steer clear of premature death and ensure that they experience their full fate.

Besides the types of ancestors and deaths, there are different levels of ancestors. Some people die honorably, while others are not fit to be regarded as honorable ancestors. Non-honorable ancestors are not eligible for worship after death. Those who are worshiped must have lived by certain standards and levels of existence in their lifetime. Honorable ancestors who make it past a certain level of living become disconnected from their loved ones once they die and become worshiped. These individuals are symbolic of the passage between the realms of the living and the dead. The behaviors, values, manners, and morals that a person exhibits during their lifetime are what determine their eligibility for veneration when they pass. If they prove to be respectable, an invocation is conducted upon their death, so their energy materializes. When this happens, the person becomes a messenger that all people, not just their friends and family, can worship.

This is why Yorubas strive to be and do good things and don't accept people who exhibit unwanted behavior. They understand that every moment in their lives counts when it comes to ensuring veneration after death. Ancestors are spiritual representations of important concepts, such as development, growth, creation, and community. They are also emblematic of harmony, balance, amity, and peace. We turn to our ancestors whenever we need guidance and seek a sense of direction in life. If you're close enough to your ancestor, you can encourage them to fight for you and direct you toward places and opportunities that are in your best interest. Yorubas believe that ancestors are powerful enough to shape our futures because they're the ones responsible for mapping out our fates. There is no better force to ask for orientation and attain a better sense of direction than our ancestors. Building a strong connection with them is a surefire way to easily overcome the obstacles we face.

# Different Types of Egun

1. **Egun Iya or Egun Baba:** These ancestors are immediate family members.
2. **Egun Idile:** The souls of non-immediate family members. They are ancestors that we're related to or have a blood connection with.
3. **Eleye or Aje:** These are believed to be the souls of witches.
4. **Abiku:** The souls of children who either die young or during childbirth.
5. **Egun Ilu:** The ancestors who founded communities, cities, towns, tribes, clans, etc.
6. **Ebora:** The lava and fire spirits.
7. **Oso:** These ancestors were native medicine men and warlords during their lifetime.
8. **Egun Enia Sasa:** The ancestors who were once popular, renowned, or famous or served as priests or priestesses.
9. **Egun Igi:** The souls who live in trees.
10. **Egun Gun Olufe:** Ancestors who used to be Babalawos.

11. **Egun Eleko:** The spirits of the friends you made and acquaintances you met in your past lives.

# The Basics of Working with Ancestors

To reach out to your ancestors, you must first say an oath for your well-being. Your undertaking can be recited in your own language and style; *however you like*. If you wish to make great transformations in your life, you need to seek the help of a professional Babalawo, as they are already aligned with this energy. In order to manifest the spirit of the ancestors, you must represent them through certain rituals and costumes. Priests and priestesses are typically the mediums used to invoke ancestors.

There is neither a right nor wrong time to worship your ancestors. You don't need to wait for calamities to happen to start working on building a connection with your ancestors. However, there are some signs that suggest that ancestor worship is long overdue. For instance, if you notice that there are unhealthy habits, such as smoking, drinking, or gambling, or certain illnesses and chronic diseases, like heart conditions, cancer, or even mental conditions running in the family, then it's time to reach out to your ancestors. Negative repetitive events and situations are also signs that you need to work with your ancestors. Worshiping them allows you to get rid of generational troubles and problems and can help you stop them from being passed down to future generations.

Some practitioners think that the experience that results from worshiping their ancestors is highly spiritual and that it transcends the worldly aspect of religion. There are two main ways in which one can worship the ancestors and appease them; making offerings of items that they enjoyed in their lifetime or cleaning their graves. Some people like to invite people over for dinner and dedicate the entire gathering to a deceased loved one. Regularly visiting your ancestors' graves and lighting up candles for them is also a highly appreciated act of worship.

# How It Works

Yoruba beliefs distinguish between a person's biological genes and physical body and spiritual genes and astral body. When we are born into the world, we are granted our allotted physical body, and our genes are given to us by our parents. They are, however, not responsible for the astral aspects of our being. Our spiritual selves are influenced by our ancestors and are left behind in the spiritual realm even after our journey into the physical world begins. Our astral aspect stays behind because it keeps our physical bodies connected to the spiritual world and ensures that we don't get too involved in earthly matters. Our souls are supposed to remind us of the importance of partaking in spiritual activities, guiding us back whenever we want to visit the spirit world.

Since our souls, which are essentially linked to our ancestors, oversee our lives in the physical world, we can get rid of obstacles and achieve a more harmonious life by worshiping our ancestors. Another reason why Yorubas are attuned to their ancestors is they are constantly aware that the present moment is no more than a mere continuation of past events and that it is also an antecedent and a determinant of the future.

It's not a problem if your ancestors aren't buried anywhere near your home or even if you don't know where they're buried. What's more important than their physical location is recognizing that your body is a vessel of their biological and spiritual genetics and part of their physical and astral bodies. Our ancestors are always with us, no matter what we're doing and wherever we go, which is why you should let your intuition guide you when you're praying to your ancestors and working with them. When you pray to your ancestors, you're not only honoring them, but you're also asking them for things that you wish they could help you with. You can ask them for guidance, abundance, health, good fortune, and more. Open your prayers with something like,

> *"You, my ancestors, promised me a life of (abundance, good fortune, happiness, etc.), so bring the (abundance, good fortune, happiness, etc.) of this world into my life."*

Some practitioners prefer to pray to their ancestors at the place of worship to which they belong. Don't feel ashamed if you're reaching out to your ancestor to ask them for something. Recognizing their power and trusting that they can influence your life for the better is one of the best forms of veneration. The worst thing you can do is not remember them, recognize their power, or ask them for anything at all.

## How to Reach Out to Your Ancestors

There are no guidelines you need to adhere to in order to successfully reach out to your ancestors. This is a very personal and intimate endeavor that should be guided by your relationship with your loved ones before they pass. Learn their preferences, know what your wishes are, and use your intuition. That said, it's normal if you don't know where to begin, which is why we are here to suggest a few things you can do to start building a connection with your ancestors.

### Don't Hesitate to Talk to Them

If you wish to start working with your ancestors, you have to let go of any social constructs and worries that you have. This is about you and your relationship with your ancestor, which is why you should start clearing your mind and shifting your attention toward connecting with your deceased loved one. It's normal to feel awkward talking to the dead and working with them. If you decide to share your beliefs with anyone, you'll likely encounter people who think you're crazy, suggest that you're dabbling in demonic activities, or call you a witch. Release all your fears and understand that this is something that you have to do. You don't need to share your convictions with anyone unless you're ready to do so.

We all have masculine and feminine energies, and the parts of ourselves that can communicate with the dead happen to be feminine. This is because these energies are generally calmer, more receptive, and popular for their intuitiveness. Don't hesitate to lean into your feminine energy and listen to emotions like compassion and empathy. Learn to let go of unhealthy notions you may have, such as toxic masculinity.

If you're susceptible to reaching out to the dead, know that they will not harm you. You have nothing to worry about as long as you set strong and clear boundaries with your divine self and the spiritual realm and only reach out to the ones you're sure to have your best interest at heart. Consult a Babalawo or call on a protector guide before you begin. They can guide your prayers and rituals and ensure that you don't attract any low-vibrational or unwanted spirits into your life. Your protector guide can be any animal spirit guide or archangel that you're used to working with.

You have to accept that dark spirits exist and that not all of your ancestors have your best interest in mind. However, you shouldn't let this scare you away from connecting with souls who can guide you. You can transform your life by working with your ancestors if you take the right precautions and set clear boundaries.

### Explore Family Traditions

Your journey will naturally be different from others because each person has unique family traditions. Working with your ancestors should be a personalized and unique process, which is why you shouldn't blindly copy what anyone else is doing, even if it feels safer. You must explore your cultural and family traditions to work with your ancestors. Your intuition is key, as well. You'll need all the help you can get at first, so you should try to speak to as many family members as possible. Talk to them about your ancestors, and if they're spiritual individuals, you can ask them if they have any rituals and prayers that they can pass on to you.

Learn about your ancestor's preferences, the activities they used to enjoy in their spare time, the food they liked to eat, what their spiritual beliefs were, what their veneration practices looked like, etc. Any information you get can help you strengthen your bond with your ancestors, understand how to reach out to them, and find out what your offerings should be. However, if you believe that they don't resonate with you and your intuition, you shouldn't force them into your practice. You won't succeed if you aren't fully convinced or don't feel comfortable with what you're doing. Remember that this is a shared bond between you and your ancestors.

Exploring your traditions and working your way up the family tree is an act of worship itself. You'll find it challenging to retrace your roots, especially if you encounter generational challenges and traumas in the process. Don't let this discourage you, and remind yourself that the process counts as an honorable intention. The more you familiarize yourself with your ancestors, the more easily you'll be able to call on their spirits and express your appreciation.

If you don't live in the land of your ancestors, you'll benefit significantly from going back to their homeland and learning about their cultural traditions. Get to know the elders who currently live there, as they'll be future ancestors. Find out about their rituals and veneration practices (if any), and ask them if they can pass on their traditions to you.

### Pay Equal Attention to the Living Elders

You don't need to wait until members of your family move on to the spiritual realm so you can start working with them. You can still venerate living elders in your family and honor them. They are technically your ancestors too, which means that you're still doing spiritual work. Working with your ancestors during their lifetimes makes it easier to bond with them in the afterlife, as you've already established the basis of your connection.

Honoring your living elders is one way to honor the ancestors and to continue to bond with them after they pass.

https://unsplash.com/photos/uGDH9jS9bfo

You shouldn't hesitate to reach out to the ones you weren't close to in your lifetime. You should still give it a go even if you've never met them before. Worst case scenario, they won't respond to your efforts. This usually happens if the person never ever even made it to the other side, wasn't spiritual, or just didn't believe in these things. However, in most cases, they will. Even though you don't need to have a direct relationship with your elders to be able to connect with them after they die, it does help to have a pre-existing bond with them. This allows you to call them in, and you can align with their energy faster.

Besides, you can stimulate generational healing and diffuse years of traumas by working with your living elders. Have them tell you their stories and experiences- the good, bad, joyful, and painful. By doing so, you can help them relieve some of the burdens they carry before they pass onto the spiritual realm.

### Call Their Spirits In

If you want to boost the effectiveness of your spiritual work, you should consider building an ancestral altar and consulting a Babalawo for specialized ritual work and prayers. Once you're ready, call your ancestors in by leaving them their preferred offerings on your shrine. These can include some of their possessions, favorite food, beverages they liked, and even promises. Your altar should be tailored to the needs and desires of the ancestor that you're working with, as this can help you strengthen your connection with your ancestors. Carefully selecting your offerings also shows them that you appreciate them and are determined to build a connection with them.

Besides praying to your ancestors, you should also call to your ancestors as you meditate. Meditation allows you to enter a trance or altered state of consciousness, making it easier to align with their energies and quickly feel their existence. You can spend as much time as you like (typically between 10 to 30 minutes) calling any ancestor you wish to work with. Work with ancestors to whom you feel most connected and build on your efforts from there. Lighting candles makes it a lot easier to interact with spirits, so choose candles in their favorite colors. Don't forget to celebrate their birthdays and other important events.

Now that you've read this chapter, you'll understand how to work with your ancestors and how this endeavor works. Read the following chapter to find out how you can enhance your Ori with the help of your deceased loved ones.

# Chapter 7: Living with the Blessings of Ancestors

Improving your Ori and working with your ancestors is a two-way relationship. You need to strengthen your Ori and work with it before you can try to reach out to them. Worshiping your Ori can help you strengthen your intuition and enhance your connection with the spiritual realm, making it easier to enter a trance state of consciousness and communicate with your ancestors. You can ask them to help you improve your connection with your highest self or Ori. With their guidance and wisdom, you'll be able to grasp a deeper understanding of your authentic self and the purpose of your existence.

By reading this chapter, you'll learn how to build and work with an ancestor shrine. You'll also learn how to conduct ancestral visualization. Finally, you'll find out how ancestral meditation can help you understand the role that you play in the world.

## Building an Ancestor Shrine

Ifa Yorubas believe that a person draws the power that allows them to invoke and work with spirits during the initiation ritual and the training period that follows. The only exception, however, is connecting with an ancestor spirit. According to this belief system, we all have the innate ability to bond with our blood relatives, even if they've passed onto the spiritual realm. It doesn't matter if we've been initiated into the practice or not, which just proves how intimate and powerful this connection is. It is your birthright to get to know your ancestors and ask for their guidance and support.

Creating a shrine for your ancestors and placing offerings is important.
*https://unsplash.com/photos/GRI_6wnQjjs*

We bond with our ancestors every day without even noticing it. Cooking a recipe the way your great-grandmother made it or asking yourself what your grandfather would have done when you're at a crossroads in life are all examples of subtle ancestral communications. Direct interactions are also commonly made during dreams and when one participates in ancestor celebrations and festivals.

Since annual ancestor festivals are not prevalent in Western countries, many practitioners build altars and use them as the center of their spiritual activities. Building an Egun altar can get anywhere from very simple to highly intricate. Complex shrines, however, require extensive training to build and maintain. The most common traditional Yoruba ancestor shrine requires you to bury your ancestor under your home, so the tomb serves as the foundation. Since the chances are that you won't be able to do that, you can use basic traditional elements to construct your shrine.

Use the information you gathered about your ancestors, along with your intuition, to determine how you should go about the process. You can also incorporate spiritual items like an Opa Egun and an Egun pot to strengthen your efforts and improve your connection and ability to communicate with them. To do that, you'd have to consult a professional Orisha priest to find out which traditional items can be beneficial for your practice. You also need their guidance to prepare them correctly. Once you have all the basic elements put together, you can contact your ancestor to determine whether they would like you to add anything else to the shrine.

# Basics of Setting Up an Ancestor or Egun Shrine

### Prepare Your Space

Find a quiet and comfortable space to build your altar. Clean it thoroughly and organize the area around it. You should keep your altar as clean and tidy as possible after you build it because dirt and clutter can attract low-vibrational spirits. The environment around you mirrors your inner state of mind. Your home can either support your efforts toward change or hinder your journey toward growth. Ifa beliefs suggest that you should tidy your home up if you feel confused or overwhelmed. While this will not make all your problems disappear, it will give you some clarity about the situation.

Smudge your room after you've cleaned and organized it. A large seashell is typically used for this process. If you don't have one, you can light up some leaves in a clay pot or any other fireproof container. Make sure that the container you use is only used for the purpose of smudging. Use a feather or your hand to fan the smoke as you move and circulate the container around the room. Sage and cedar leaves are most popularly used for smudging traditions, as they're very aromatic and cleansing. You can use other types of leaves if those aren't available. Adding incense to the container can also boost the effectiveness of smudging.

Place your ingredients in a pile in the center of the fireproof container and say a prayer directly as you start to smudge the area) Be clear about your intentions of cleansing the room and dispersing any unwanted spirits. You can recite the prayer in any language you want. Start by paying your respects to the spirit of the ancestors, say your name and state your lineage, bless the spirit of the leaves, and then ask it to do something for you. You can ask it to attract good fortune, peace, stability, and wisdom. When you're ready, conclude your prayers by thanking the spirit of the leaves.

Use a match to light the smudge and wait for the flame to die down and leave a cloud of smoke behind. Move around the room, ensuring that the smoke spreads around. As you do that, focus on your intentions and smudge the rest of your home. Keep in mind that if you allow your mind to wander off and let intrusive thoughts take over, this will defeat the entire purpose of the process. After you've smudged your space, cleanse yourself with the smoke. Start at your feet and move up the front of your body. Cleanse your head and move down your back.

To keep the effects of the smudging practice, you need to seal the space. There are several types of seals that you can use. However, the easiest one, especially if you're uninitiated, involves water, fragrance, and body fluids. Fill up a bowl with water and add a few drops of a fragrance that you frequently wear. You should also add a small amount of urine or saliva to the mixture. This asserts to the ancestor spirits that you are in charge of any communications that take place.

Speak the names of the ancestors that you don't wish to communicate with – along with the reasons why you don't want them to participate – before you seal your space. If you don't know your ancestors by name, you can alternatively express the problems and behaviors that aren't welcome in your space. You should exclude ancestors who have committed suicide, died brutal or traumatic deaths, were physically abusive, engaged in sexual abuse, or suffered from addiction or substance abuse. Make sure to protect yourself from any potentially harmful influences and get rid of any possibilities before you seal the space.

Speak a prayer (similar to the one you made to the smudge) directly into the water. Then, sprinkle the water (using your left hand) all over the space that you cleaned using the smudge. Focus on your intention throughout the process.

### Set Up and Use the Shrine

You're only ready to set up the shrine after you've cleaned and sealed it. Your altar should be a space of remembrance for your ancestors. Dedicate it to the elders who have added to your life and improved it through their wisdom and guidance. You can also use it to communicate with other deceased relatives or any popular figure or mentor who has inspired you, even if they aren't related to you.

Set up a table and place a white cover or cloth over it in your designated area. Decorate it with white candles, some of their possessions, items that they enjoyed in their lifetime, drawings or pictures of them, and a glass of water. The best thing about Ifa and Yoruba practices is that they welcome various spiritual and individual differences. Indigenous practitioners dedicate their altars to prophets and historical figures of different religions and backgrounds. For instance, if your ancestor was a devout Catholic, you can place a rosary or a Bible on the altar.

When everything's ready, light up one of the candles and stand in front of your shrine. Make a promise to your ancestors that you'll be using the shrine regularly for prayers, remembrance, and meditation. You should also provide offerings for them frequently. You don't need to promise to use it every day or three times a week if you know that you won't be able to live up to that type of commitment. However, if you agree to use it three times a month, you shouldn't break your promise. It's better to start slowly and steadily and work your way up than to make and break a promise that you can't handle. Otherwise, you'd be proving to your ancestors that you aren't serious about working with them and building a connection. While your ancestors will be happy to help you when you encounter challenges in your path, you should avoid turning to them only when you need them. This weakens the bond you have with them. It's a bit like only saying prayers when you want something.

Remember your ancestors and identify the ways in which they affected you and influenced your perceptions. Think of the influences you wish to keep and strengthen and the ones you want to eliminate. Meditate on all the positive characteristics that your deceased loved ones possessed. Were they helpful, wise, courageous, creative, strong, or honest? Which of their qualities do you want them to pass on to you? The stronger your connection with your ancestor grows, the easier you'll be able to call them into your day-to-day life whenever you need them to bless you with a specific quality. For example, when you don't know which decision to make, you can call on a certain ancestor because they're known for their wisdom. If a situation requires you to think outside of the box, you can call on the creative spirit. Every time you remember an ancestor and think about how they would have acted in a certain situation, you are communicating with them and engaging in the form of worship. When you've made your promise and meditated, end your session by thanking your ancestors for their wisdom and positive qualities.

## Ancestral Visualization

Switch some soft lights on, light up a few candles, and sit by your altar. Make sure you have pictures of your ancestors put up, along with a few personal elements and cultural objects if you don't already. Burn incense, take a moment to express your gratitude, and gather all your attention toward this process. Thank your ancestors for granting you the opportunity to be in this world and honor their existence.

Draw in a deep breath and visualize all your thoughts evaporating from your mind. Once your mind is clear, start your ancestral visualization practice. Visualize yourself in a large, alluring field or any other place in nature. Allow yourself to feel safe in this space. It should be welcoming and familiar. Imagine all the details of the place, including how the grass or earth feels beneath your feet, the chilly breeze caressing your skin, and the smell of fresh air mixed with the subtle aroma of flowers. Try to make your imagination feel as real as possible. Once you feel like you're truly a part of your visualization, focus on your intention to meet an ancestor. Express the desire of wanting to connect with them. You can either choose a specific ancestor or open yourself to the collective and see who comes to you.

If you're struggling with making your visualization feel real, you can recognize it as a portion of your imagination and bring your consciousness into the process. That said, most people find the practice more effective when it feels real. The more you practice this visualization, the easier it will be to involve your senses and emotions.

When your ancestor shows up, start asking them questions. Allow your curiosity to take the lead, and don't worry too much about putting them on the stand or coming off as judgmental. Your ancestor is here to help and guide you. They will not necessarily tell you exactly what you need to do to fix a problem. However, they'll likely give you some advice or share a story that will help direct you toward the right path. Flexibility and openness are key here. Carefully listen and interpret their words as they speak. Once they've finished talking to you, thank them and take your time to exit the meditation and return to reality. You should regularly express your gratitude and pray to the ancestors that show up in your meditations because this helps you maintain a strong bond with them and shows them that you honor and appreciate their help.

## Ancestral Meditation

Sit comfortably near your altar and draw in several deep breaths to clear your mind. This meditation is more effective when listened to because it guides your subconscious mind when you enter a trance state. You can ask someone you trust to read it to you. Alternatively, you can record your voice and play it to yourself whenever you read it. Either way, the words should be spoken softly, clearly, and slowly.

Relax your body and listen to the person guiding the meditation as they count down from 13. Don't imagine the numbers; just follow the voice of the guide. Start visualizing a giant tree. This tree is larger than anything you've ever seen. Tell yourself that this is the World Tree- the bridge between the realms of the physical and the spiritual. Think of the pictures in your mind as a portal that you can journey through. Bring yourself into the picture and imagine yourself passing through the doorway of your mind. Stand in front of the tree.

Listen to the sound of the leaves and the branches as the wind passes through them. Inhale the smell of the earth right after it has rained. Extend your arms and touch the monumental bark of the tree. With your hands there, focus strongly on the intention of calling on an ancestor spirit. Express your wish for them to help you bring balance and harmony to the world.

Move along the tree and keep observing its roots until you find an opening. Release all your fears and jump into the gap in the tree. You'll find a tunnel leading downward. Follow the spiral until you see a flickering light - much like a fire - at the end of the tunnel. Approach it.

The tunnel leads to a forest clearing with a huge fire in the center of it. The spirits of the ancestors are gathered around it. Some of them are dancing, while others are just observing it. Don't walk toward them. Stand by the trees at the edge and patiently wait for an ancestor to come to you. It may be someone you know well, a blood relative you heard or know of, or an ancestor of spirit that you don't know at all. If you don't know the spirit who approached you, simply introduce yourself to them.

Ask them about your purpose in the world and also ask for their guidance on how to make your world a better place. Try to learn more about what you need to do to make the world more harmonious and peaceful. Ask them for advice and wisdom you can live by and any other questions you have.

Your ancestor might offer you a gift that will put you on the right path. The purpose of the gift can also be to help you remember key aspects of your conversation. Take a moment of introspection to think of what you can offer them in return. Don't stress about it much but follow your intuition. When the conversation comes to an end, thank your ancestors for their guidance and step away.

Start searching for the tunnel and step through it. Follow the spiral as it spirals upward and leads you to the base of the tree. When you step out, rest your hand on the bark of the World Tree and thank it for making this journey possible. Step through the doorway of your mind and slowly shift your awareness to reality. The person guiding this meditation should signal that it's time to come back to the time and place of reality. Open your eyes whenever you're ready.

Now that you have read this chapter, you are ready to start living with the blessings of your ancestors. Read the following chapter to learn all about heavenly mates and how they can aid one's Ori.

# Chapter 8: Egbe, Your Spiritual Family

This chapter is dedicated to a unique group of spirits called Egbe Orun. By reading it, you'll learn who these spirits are, their characteristics, and how to appease them through their preferred offerings. You'll understand how they influence your life and how they can help you with various aspects of spiritual communication, including your alignment with your Ori.

## Who Are the Egbe Orun?

The Egbe Orun, also known as Alaragbo, Egberun, and simply Egbe, is a group of spirits who have served as companions for humans since the beginning of time. Their name is derived from the Yoruba word Egbe, which means *"heavenly spirit"* or *"astral mates."* According to the Yoruba people, every person on Earth has a comrade who lives in the heavenly realm. This belief is based on the idea that each soul comes from heaven and eventually returns there. People living on earth are the personification of their own spirit in a physical body. Olodumare created the souls, and Obatala molded a physical body for them. As Olodumare made the physical bodies come to life, he gave them two souls. One traveled back to the spiritual realm, while the other remained in the body.

People often see their spiritual counterpart in their dreams, whether it looks like them or someone else. Since both souls share a history, they know more about each other than unrelated souls. The two souls are identical and are able to find each other. However, Egbe are believed to be more powerful spirits than their earthly counterparts because they aren't polluted with the demands of the physical body.

According to Yoruba beliefs, one of the souls stays behind in the spiritual world to keep its twin tethered to it. This allows people to visit this realm whenever they wish to journey there or seek guidance from one of its inhabitants. Egbe also watches over their earthly counterpart, safeguarding them. Whenever an earthly soul veers off its path, its twin will remind them of its spiritual nature. Tapping into this unique bond with our heavenly mate is also a great reminder that our time in this realm is only temporary.

Because people have different characteristics, their connection with their twin souls also differs. This also affects their higher level of consciousness, which is reached through spiritual intuition. Those who have a strong bond with their Egbe are more frequently influenced by these spirits. They don't even need to put in much effort to reach the spiritual realm, yet their messages will be heard loud and clear. They allow themselves to be led by their spiritual intuition and communicate with Egbe, hoping to reach a spiritual awakening. The Egbe, in turn, send their messages back through dreams or visualization and divination practices. They can also cause objects to disappear from one's physical environment and others to appear. These are actions the Egbe uses to send specific messages which can only be understood by the twin soul. However, the Egbe will only provide their blessing, protection, and guidance if they're properly appeased. By learning to placate the Egbe and forming a bond with them, you'll be able to fulfill your soul's destiny.

## Types of Egbe Orun

The ancient Yoruba people learned about the existence of heavenly mates through practices involving spiritual communication. As they started associating themselves with the spiritual world, they learned that the Egbe behave very similarly to humans. They live in communities organized based on beliefs, preferences, and characters. Some of the behavior displayed by these astral souls reminded the Yoruba of their own behavior from when they were children. It's believed that children still remember their twin souls but forget them as they become adults.

To this day, Yoruba practitioners actively communicate with the heavenly communities through different oracular practices and tools. They've identified different types of Egbe traits and societies, but there are many more that remain unknown. Below are some of the major groups of Egbe Orun.

## Eléékò

The Eléékò is a colorful group with many different types of personalities. Their moods are changeable, and they're often led by their desires. They're typically patient, but when angered, they show no mercy and are hard to appease. This contrasting behavior is very similar to that of Esu, a shapeshifting spirit and trickster deity known for his many mischiefs. Eléékò is also intelligent and can be very creative, especially when it comes to sending messages and playing tricks. They can be sneaky, and their loyalty can shift very rapidly.

The Eléékò are known to steal valuable belongings. This is a clear sign that they spend time around a person. However, they only steal from those who have more than enough or have disrespected them, the Egbe, or other inhabitants of the spiritual world. The Eléékò will share their bounty with the less fortunate as a punishment or a lesson. Children of the Yoruba community who exhibit this behavior are thought to be members of the Eléékò. Any child who is stubborn, steals, or is overly talkative has to undergo a specific ritual. Otherwise, they'll grow up to be just like Eléékò.

## Ìyálóde

The Ìyálóde is another large Egbe group. They are natural-born leaders and are often compared to leaders in society in the physical realm. While powerful, they're only considered leaders in the eyes of the souls living on the earth. Their society is named after Ìyálóde, a female leader who initially led the Yoruba to believe that the group has only female members. After further exploration, Yoruba practitioners learned that both men and women could be Ìyálóde.

Members of the Iyalode come in all shapes, sizes, and ages. They behave as leaders do. They're organized and motivated and can inspire others. They take care of themselves and dress nicely, which makes them easily noticeable. They like to show off even when sending messages, but they're also charitable. That said, it's not suggested that you anger them. Because they can be just as malicious with their punishment as they are generous with their blessings, the Ìyálóde are

70

known to pay particular attention to children and do everything they can to protect them and their parents or guardians. Those who harm children have every reason to fear the Ìyálóde as their punishment is exceptionally harsh.

## Baálè

Baálè is another talented group known to exhibit both the leadership skills of Ìyálóde and the colorful traits of Eléékò. Their name in Yoruba means "*the tribe's ruler.*" This name was given to them after the Yoruba discovered their qualities and virtues.

Their nature sets them apart from other Egbe groups, and they are often considered too domineering. Despite this, the Yoruba believe that the Baálè is one of the most straightforward Egbe groups. They often turn to them for divination or judgment. That said, one needs to be very careful when communicating with the Baálè as they are known to issue harsh punishment, especially when it comes to deviant behavior.

## Asípa

The Asípa are another group that's very vocal in expressing their intentions and needs. As straightforward as they may seem, they aren't always truthful either. Sometimes, they hide their true intentions behind a grand display of false devotion and allegiance, which speaks about their disloyal nature. Not only that, but conveniently for them, they are often forgetful - especially when it comes to an untruth they've said. They can also cause temporary or permanent memory loss for earthly souls, which hinders their ability to fulfill their density.

Their influence on people makes them forget their encounter or talk so much they make a person dizzy. If one has a feeling that they've met the person they're talking to before - despite meeting them the first time they are likely a member of the Asípa society. You may also mistrust them instinctively without knowing why. The Asípa will often act against people who reject their fate or whose souls are meant to become Egbe but refused. The Yoruba believe that in addition to hindering people's destiny, the Asípa can also exchange people's fates. According to this idea, by appeasing this Egbe group, one can find a different, better path for themselves.

## Jagun

Also known as Jagunjagun, Jagun is an Egbe society named after a warrior of the same name. Similar to their namesake, Jagun are known to be persistent and relentless in their pursuits. They're highly adaptable and accommodating and know what it takes to reach their goal. They don't like to waste their time on mindless activities or pleasantries, even to appease someone else.

Jagun are typically identified as children who exhibit very unusual behavior. Instead of acting infantile, these children are uptight and meticulous from an early age. This behavior is noticeable even in babies who don't cry much and patiently wait until the adults can tend to their needs. Adult Jagun can be promiscuous, but they're usually good at covering it up with seemingly model behavior.

### Olúgbógeró

The Olúgbógeró is a group with a fluid nature, with its members having multifaceted personalities. They're free as the rivers and other flowing waters, and their characters can't be influenced. One behavior they can't be dissuaded from is carrying a piece of cloth on or near their body. Besides water, the Olúgbógeró are also associated with stillborn children. These are believed to be souls whose fate was influenced by malicious forces, such as curses. Consequently, they're left without the physical body they were meant to be born into.

### Móohún

Móohún is a very defiant group of Egbe who don't care about following rules, helping others, or even making decisions. They also exhibit other childlike behavior like stubbornness and forgetfulness. Because of this, they were believed to be a group of children who couldn't be trusted with any critical task. They're unlikely to be relied on or help with any issue when called upon. The only thing they'll happily spend time on is making themselves look good.

### Adétayànyá

Adétayànyá is a strange group consisting of children. They share similarities with Oro, Egunguns brother. Some even believe they are related to him. One of their most prominent characteristics is their reverence for refuse dumps. They either seek out even the most secluded dumps or greet the ones they pass on their travels. Adétayànyá spends a lot of their time at the dumpsites.

# Honoring Egbe Orun

The Egbe is traditionally venerated through offerings, rites, and prayers, which are good ways to appease them. However, if angered, some Egbe will require spiritual sacrifices. For the Yoruba, the highest form of spiritual sacrifice is self-discipline. They use several self-discipline methods to build connections with their spiritual self and guides, including the Egbe. The Egbe, in turn, appreciate people's efforts to maintain their relationship with their heavenly mates and treasure their bond. If you wish to connect to an Egbe, you must prove to them that you are ready to form a strong bond with them and continue to reinforce it.

Building a shrine for an Egbe is a great way to honor them. Adorn it with a white cloth and red and white decorations. You'll be able to call on them to this sacred space, so make sure you set it up where you can work with them without interruptions. Egbe communicate through different means, including dreams and ocular prescriptions (causing visions). You'll also want to be able to hold bonfires near your sacred place or have a river or tree where you can leave your offerings. You can leave them organic foods like plantain, sugarcane, honey, shea butter, coconut, palm oil, kola nuts, as well as fresh water and alcohol. They also accept cheese, roasted or cooked groundnuts, a paste of yam, maize, or steamed white beans, sweet maize, beans, and yam.

# Influence of Egbe Orun

Like human societies, the various Egbe groups have different influences over the spiritual realm and earthly souls. Those who carry bad news are considered taboos, which are traditionally carried down to generations within the same family, community, or society. These are thought to cause an imbalance in one's life, such as nightmares and other cognitive disturbances. Those who want to ascertain whether an Egbe is trying to communicate with them through nightmares will need to visit an oracle.

Other Egbe have very positive influences over their earthly counterparts. They forge a strong bond with them, allowing the person to rely on them as they navigate their way through life. Some feel the need to always consult their Egbe before making an important decision. Others will even form romantic relationships with their spiritual counterparts, which often causes them to remain alone in the physical world. Egbe can be very possessive and will try to keep away other potential partners, sometimes even by causing their death. According to Yoruba traditions, a human bride and groom must always confirm they have no arrangement with their heavenly mates before they marry. They will visit an oracle who can confirm this. The priests will conduct a rite that leads to the dissolution of the spiritual arrangement that has been previously made.

If contacted by their Egbe counterpart, one must ensure their twin doesn't have any harmful tendencies. Otherwise, they'll never be able to work in unison, and the Egbe will work against the person instead. If, after consulting an oracle, a person discovers that their heavenly twin is wicked, they are advised to sever this connection as soon as possible. Sometimes these influences aren't spotted or dealt with in time because they are taught to the infantile phase many children grow to. However, when influenced by a wicked Egbe, insolent children often become unruly adults. They will get into conflicts with their peers and will never trust others. The Egbe will continue to influence them by making valuable items disappear from their community, causing further issues between them and the rest of their community.

Never ignore the Egbe, not even the good-natured groups, as they can be angered. If they are, they'll block any blessings you may receive. If the Egbe is truly upset, they'll put obstacles onto your path, making it challenging for you to obtain your goals. Sometimes, a person ignores an Egbe because they aren't aware of their messages. If that happens, the Egbe will still punish them. Those who suffer an unexplained misfortune are advised to visit an oracle and see if their problems are caused by an upset Egbe.

Developing your spiritual intuition is a great way to ensure you'll never ignore their presence or messages. The more you communicate with the Egbe Orun, the stronger your relationships become, and the more heightened your intuition will be. Learning to ask your heavenly mate for guidance, protection, and spiritual healing can teach you how to use your Ori.

# Chapter 9: Odu Ifa, a Guide to Righteous Living

Odu Ifa, the sacred scripture of the Yoruba, contains instructions for righteous living, which is one of the fundamental steps toward spiritual alignment. From this chapter, you'll learn how it was created and how it's structured, including its summary called the 16 Truths of Ifa. You'll also learn the underlying messages behind each truth and how to follow them to establish an honorable life for yourself.

## Odu Ifa

As the number of people to whom Olodumare and Obatala gave life grew, the supreme creator realized that some common issues occur in human communities. The Orishas had given Olodumare reports about illnesses, losses of property and other money troubles, fears of impending death, and many other obstacles humans faced throughout their lives. In order to help counteract the negative influences that lead to these issues, Olodumare created a decree that contained all the problems and their solutions. Among the resolutions was cherishing what people have, including family, health and overcoming illnesses, life (especially those who live long lives), children, financial security, and creativity to prevent losses. The problems he found a resolution for were presented in a prophecy containing thousands of verses and organized into 256 sections. They were transcribed in a holy text, which, for the Yoruba, embodies the sacred essences of Ifa, including destiny, truth, life, and the ultimate destination of one's soul. The knowledge of the prophecy was first given to Orunmila, the Orisha with divinatory abilities, who also acted as the first Babalawo (priest) in Ife. At first, people came to Orunmila with their issues, as he was the only one who could look into their destiny. However, Olodumare and Orunmila believed this power shouldn't be left in the hands of one person, even one as powerful as the Orishas.

According to the lore, Orumnila learned to decipher the messages of the 16 Truths of Ifa after he married his second wife, Odu. His first wife, Egan, couldn't give him any children. He asked Olodmare what to do and was advised to marry Odu, so Egan would give him children. When Orunmila married Odu, Egan was able to bear 16 children, who are also considered to be the children of Odu. These children grew up to be the next generation of priests and priestesses, to whom Orumila passed down the prophecy of the 256 signatures. The 16 children of Orunmila used this knowledge to help people resolve common issues, lead a balanced life, and obtain spiritual enlightenment. They were often called upon by the King of Ife to resolve conflicts and other problems occurring in his dominion.

A story that illustrates how following the prophecy brings a happier life revolves around the youngest child of Orunmila, Eji-Ogbe. On one occasion, when the King of Ife asked for their assistance, his other siblings (lcd by Ofun-Meji) left Eji-Ogbe behind. When consulting the prophecy, he learned that he should go after his sibling. He was also warned not to overlook anyone asking for assistance along the way. The other siblings weren't aware of this prophecy. When they were asked for help by the King of the Forest, they declined, saying they needed to help the King of Ife first. However, when they asked for directions to the castle of the Ife King, they were given the wrong ones and got lost. Eji-Ogbe, on the other hand, helped the King of the Forest first, and as a reward, he was given the proper directions. He reached the King of Ife before his siblings, helped him, and was given a distinguished status. When they arrived and realized their mistake, his siblings were ashamed of overlooking both Eji-Ogbe and the King of the Forest.

The children of Orunmila also passed down the prophecy to the next generation of priests and priestesses of Ifa. To this day, fully initiated Yoruba priests and priestesses learn all 256 signatures of the script. The signatures serve as a divination system used every time a Yoruba turns to their priests or priestess with a physical or spiritual problem. The diviner looks into the prophecy and determines what the sufferer needs to do to resolve their issue. Those initiated as devotees don't need to learn 256 signatures, but they're advised to follow the 16 Truths of Ifa. Upon initiation, devotees become the children of Orunmila. They can call on him for spiritual guidance, alignment, and help to reach or change their destiny. If they follow the 16 Truths of Ifa, Orunmila will grant many blessings.

# The 16 Truths of Ifa

Once the verses are transcribed, the knowledge from Odu Ifa can be summarized into 16 main points, called the 16 Truths of Ifa. According to another Yoruba tale, the truths were given to 16 priests who wanted to live forever. Orunmila decided to test them by telling them that if they followed the 16 Truths of Ifa, they'll live forever and become powerful spiritual leaders. However, the priests didn't follow the 16 truths and died soon after. The Yoruba believe that many of the issues the ancient people and Orishas encountered stem from not following the truths. Apart from the one example above, there are countless other tales about people facing problems due to disregarding dietary restrictions, disrespecting or overlooking others, and breaking taboos.

For thousands of years, the Yoruba have lived their lives following the 16 Truths of Ifa, which helped them gather an immense amount of collective spiritual wisdom. By consulting their ancestors, anyone can tap into this knowledge and gain spiritual awareness. By following these truths yourself, you can also learn how to stay true to positive spiritual values. These values are essential for finding your destiny, changing it, and aligning yourself with every part of your Ori.

The truths passed down through generations are as follows:

1. **There is only one supreme force:** Olodumare is the single being who created all things, including the universe. He was the one who provided essence to all living beings. Sealing an intention by asking for the assistance of Olodumare is the best way to ensure it takes effect.

2. **Our universe is good:** It was created by Olodumare, whose essence is entirely uncorrupted. Therefore, the universe can't be malicious. Knowing this allows people to access memories and information from the past, present, and future without fearing being misled.

3. **You should face life's obstacles head-on:** The Yoruba believe that the Orishas who faced hurdles without fear were rewarded with spiritual enlightenment, whereas those who lived in fear suffered. Consulting with spiritual helpers will enable you to conquer the toughest challenges.

4. **Evil doesn't come from one source:** For the Yoruba, the devil (as it's called in other religions) doesn't exist - and neither does its dominion (hell). Negative influences come from an infinite number of sources, and you should be prepared to ward them off at all times.

5. **You have the right to be cherished and reach fulfillment:** Don't believe anyone who tells you that you don't deserve love or to realize your dreams. Whatever experience you had in the past, accepting your rights brings you a step closer to spiritual alignment.

6. **People are in constant transition between two realms of existence:** The first one is heaven (our soul's home, according to Ifa), and the other one is called "the marketplace" (a transitional space for souls). Death is considered good because it ends the soul's suffering in an unhealthy body, and after reincarnation, it allows the soul to start anew in a healthy body.

7. **Every fiber of your being is part of the universe:** In spirit, you are one with the universe, including all of the other creations of Olodumare. Paying attention to the creations around you and honoring them through spiritual practices leads to higher self-awareness.

8. **A person's character and personality traits determine their fate:** How your character makes you think, feel, and actions will determine the ultimate course of your fate. Good character helps you fulfill your destiny (or change it), while a bad character will hinder you in this quest.

9. **Demonstrating superiority should be avoided:** Only Ifa and Olodumare can be superior to every other being in any realm. Among people, Babalawos, and Orishas, no one is superior, and no one is above making mistakes. Blaming your mistakes on others and complaining about them because you feel superior is a sign of evil influence.

10. **Don't hurt others in any way, even if they act maliciously:** Let their malicious nature consume them instead. Causing harm will only make you miss out on all the blessings you can get from the Olodumare and the Orishas for good behavior.

11. **Nourish your connection to the universe:** Every part of the universe is sacred and must be treated respectfully. You need to pay your respect to all its benevolent spirits to keep yourself in their good favor in case you need them.

12. **Don't discriminate against others:** Every person is valuable in their own way, regardless of their personality and appearance. Being ignorant of other people's values will prevent you from obtaining spiritual abundance, and you'll remain just as powerless as those you discriminate against.

13. **Diversity is a testimony to the infinite power of the creator:** It should be celebrated because it can bring all its creations together. In people, diversity manifests in the spectrum of potentials we all possess. This allows us to choose which one we want to see come true.

14. **You are free to determine the course of your fate and choose your guardians:** Whatever fate you pick for yourself depends on you alone. The same applies to the divine guardian you pick for guidance. Offering sacrifice to the Orishas, ancestors, and other spiritual guides is an excellent way to ensure you receive the assistance you need.

15. **Divinatory practices are an excellent way to find your path:** Whenever you need advice for fulfilling or changing your destiny or having a long and prosperous life, consult Ifa, and you'll have the answers.

16. **Have a goal to gather wisdom and spiritual growth:** These are required for spiritual alignment and a balanced Ori. Prayers and other forms of spiritual discipline are fundamental for spiritual growth and honing spiritual intuition.

# Following the 16 Truths of Ifa

The truths are simple decrees anyone can follow in their daily life. Here is some advice on how to follow the 16 Truths of Ifa:

## Don't Mislead People with False Knowledge

Don't talk about something without offering verifiable information. Thinking something is true doesn't make it the absolute truth unless you and others can verify it. Only talk about what you have knowledge of, and don't mislead people with your actions and words. Otherwise, you'll spread false information about your knowledge, thoughts, and behavior. Be transparent with your feelings, and always tell people what you expect from them and what they can expect in return. Practice open-mindedness when communicating with others, and listen to them - especially when they speak of things you aren't familiar with. The same applies to rituals and ceremonies you aren't familiar with. Only perform those you practiced before and have successful experiences following through.

## Don't Pretend to Be Superior

No matter how much knowledge you've gathered throughout your life, you can always learn more. There will always be things you haven't learned yet, so don't pretend you are the source of all wisdom or that you're superior due to the knowledge you possess. Wise people never do that. Instead, they remain humble and continue learning because they are aware of the immense amount of wisdom they can still gather. They never let their egos get in their way, no matter how challenging this is at times. However, even if it feels unfair to deny satisfying your ego, you should look at this as another opportunity to learn and grow spiritually. By remaining humble, you have much better chances for self-realization.

## Always Have Good Intentions and Respect

Bad intentions have a negative influence on your spiritual well-being. They can also prevent you from spiritual communication and hinder your ability to reach alignment with your Ori and improve it. This can also be challenging, especially if others don't have good intentions toward you or don't respect your opinions. However, by taking a positive approach, you'll be able to thrive despite their disrespectful and negative disposition. Respect other people's views and actions, even if they are different from yours. Pay particular attention not to disrespect your elders or those weaker than you (physically or mentally). Your elders are far wiser than you are, and you never know when you might need their assistance. Weaker people should also be respected because their weakness is not their fault. They can contribute just as much to the spiritual health of their community as any other member. Respect the taboos and prohibitions by not breaking them, ever. Otherwise, they'll have the same effect as malicious intentions.

**Respect Your Friendships**

You'll find that if you make yourself available for your friends when they need you the most, they'll respond accordingly. Don't disrespect them by gossiping about them behind their backs or sharing a secret entrusted to you. Honor their choices regarding their life, even if you disagree with them. Respect their loved ones, just as you would want them to honor yours. Try not to advise them against a decision too frequently, and let them make their own choices.

Always respect your friendships.
https://unsplash.com/photos/X1GZqv-F7Tw

**Honor Your Sacred Space and Spiritual Tools**

The Yoruba were always vocal about keeping their sacred places (where they perform rites and ceremonies clean). You should also ensure to keep your spiritual tools clean from negative influences. This applies to the shrine, symbols, and other items you use for spiritual communication and other spiritual practices. Your body, mind, and spirit are amongst these tools, too, so don't forget to cleanse them regularly. Taking cleansing baths and asking your spiritual helpers to purify you physically and mentally can go a long way to expel all the negative energy tainting your spiritual essence and hindering you from working on your Ori.

## Adhere to All Laws

Adhering to moral and legal laws is another crucial aspect of the life of the Yoruba. Both make our communities safer, allowing everyone to live together peacefully. Good moral conduct enables you to stay true to your values and align your Ori with these as well. Remember that this is only possible if you cultivate values that adhere to commonly applied moral codes.

# Chapter 10: Aligning with Your Ori

Even though your ancestors, the Egbe, the Orishas, and other spiritual helpers can pave the way to a balanced Ori, the only true way to accomplish this is through Iwa-pele, a good character. This chapter discusses what a good character is and why you should work on improving yours. You'll also learn how to identify a bad character, techniques to improve it, and live your life in a way that your character remains good at all times.

## The Concept of Iwa-Pele

The teachings of Ifa all revolve around living an honorable life and being in good standing with other people in one's community. Iwa-pele is a concept that encompasses logical beliefs that help people live balanced lives. Essentially, according to Ifa, Iwa-pele is only an accurate description of how the world works. Unlike other belief systems, the religion of the Yoruba people has no myths and tales about miracles resolving people's problems. Instead, they have a concept that tells them how the Universe works and how they should act. It also teaches that when one behaves in alignment with the Universe, their life will be infinitely better. Olodumare created a Universe that has logical rules which keep it balanced and pure. While ebbos, sacrifices, prayers, and rites can help you manifest your intention, none will be enough if what you ask for goes against Iwa-pele.

Every person carries an essence that interacts with other people's energies. This interaction is present in every part of your life and is expressed through your behavior, speech, and thoughts. For example, if you were to steal a valuable item from someone else, they could do the same to you. Other people who see this can also steal from you, and soon none of your possessions would be safe. It's a logical chain of events caused by a force you launched by stealing. You also interact with other energies in your environment. Environmental pollution is a sign of many people being in misalignment with Iwa-pele - and one that often has dire consequences. If you don't respect natural forces, they will cause many disruptions in your life, including material losses and financial hardships. In both examples, your character sets the groundwork for the impending disaster, and it's on you to stop this from happening.

The ancient Yoruba people learned this partly from the Orishas and their own observations of how the world works. By applying common sense, they examined the negative occurrences. They concluded that Iwa-pele is a crucial tool for maintaining the balance of the Universe. According to the Yoruba, Iwa-pele does not require blind obedience to moral or legal rules. They believe that it requires spiritual intelligence, which they aim to nurture and cherish throughout their lives. Instead of obeying any divine rules, they organize their lives and act in a way that benefits them, their environment, and the Universe. It allows people to improve their lives and fulfill their destinies without hindering anyone else's.

Many of the spiritual practices of the Yoruba are based on Iwa-pele. They are designed to create unity, which further enforces people's will to behave according to the logical rules of the Universe. Most of the ceremonies require spiritual cleansing. The more people go through this in the community, the more members will start to feel closer to the Universe and each other. They become committed to demonstrating good character because they know it will improve their lives and, more importantly, do this without harming anyone else's. They know that by making choices that benefit others, they will be one step closer to spiritual fulfillment and self-realization. It's the highest blessing one can receive because it's something they've earned, and it wasn't bestowed on them by a deity or spiritual guard.

To this very day, the high priests and priestesses of Yoruba are encouraged to help anyone who asks for help. They are also taught to advise devotees to look out for people in their community and offer help whenever they can. During communal gatherings and festivities, priests and priestesses reinforce the need to spend time with family and friends and provide them with any type of support they need. They advise that you'll receive many blessings and grow personally when you demonstrate good character. Olodumare and Orunmila will grant any wishes made if these wishes are backed by a good character. If a person with good character finds themselves in trouble, they'll be more likely to receive help from others. This is probably because people with good character tend to share their good fortune with others.

Following the Yoruba example, you can also devote your time to your loved ones. You can spend quality time with them doing anything you all agree on. Sometimes just listening to each other is enough, especially if one or more of you is going through challenging times. If you can think of advice, you can offer it, but you don't need to. As long as you show unselfish interest in someone else's issue, your bond will deepen, and you'll be closer to your spiritual balance.

# Good Character and Bad Character

The name of the Iwa-pele concept is rooted in the Yoruba word Iwa, which means "*character.*" A person's character defines who they are, their essential qualities, and what makes them unique. A character can be both good and bad. Iwa-pele refers to good character. It's ascribed to a person with gentle and compassionate, and these are open-minded individuals. This is a person that respects everyone and everything in their environment. They never disrespect or overlook weaker individuals or their elders. They work with others to improve their community, which earns them great respect.

Bad character, or Iwa-buruki, on the other hand, represents the opposite of Iwa-pele. People with Iwa-buruki are disrespectful, reject other people's ideas, have a sense of superiority and don't work well with others. They often get into conflicts within their community and not only struggle to improve their lives but suffer losses and challenges in all areas of life.

The Yoruba have a fascinating tale of how good and bad characters can manifest one's destiny. In this story, Iwa is personified as a female character who became the wife of Orunmila. Before their marriage, Orunmila was advised that he would need to offer an ebbo. He was also told that he'd need to ensure Iwa remained happy after the marriage.

After making the ebbo and marrying Iwa, he did as he was told, and he had every reason to be content with his life. He was successful in everything he did, and Iwa was happy. Unfortunately, Orunmila got so comfortable in his newfound happiness that he started to neglect Iwa. He began to complain about everything she did, and suddenly no meal she prepared or chore she did was good enough for him. One day, Iwa had had enough of his complaints and left him. After this, Orunmila began to suffer one loss after another. To find out why, he went to consult with Ifa. He was told that his bad luck persisted because he hurt someone in his life, and the only way to turn things around was to ask that person to forgive him. Orunmila made an ebbo and went on a journey to find his wife. On this journey, he encountered several people who had given him clues about Iwa's whereabouts until he finally found her. With the help of a few good souls who vouched for him, he convinced her to return to him. After this, Orunmila learned never to neglect Iwa again. He also remembered all the good people who helped him along the way and started to be gentle and understanding toward them, granting them many blessings.

The moral of this story is that even if you have a good character, by turning it into a bad one, you can lose all the blessings you received before. You shouldn't overlook your character and should always ensure it's good. Had Orunmila not neglected Iwa (the personified character), he wouldn't have lost everything he did when she went away. The Yoruba believe that those who receive many blessings must have a good character.

## The Relationship between Iwa and Ori

According to the Yoruba, Iwa represents half of the personality. The other half is defined by Ori, which is the inner essence. Whereas Iwa is the outer manifestation of the personality. Iwa is what people see, and interact with, while Ori is the spiritual driving force behind the manifested behavior. When aligned with your values, Ori motivates you to display the character that protects you and carries you toward your destiny. In turn, a good character goes a long way in reinforcing an Ori with a positive disposition. Ise (skill) and Ogbon (wisdom) are two factors that affect Ori. By working on these, you can improve your Iwa. Apart from Ori, character improvement can also be inspired by Aiye (your environment) and the Orishas (through regular practice).

# The Role of Iwa-Pele in Spiritual Alignment

According to the teaching of Ifa, everyone is capable of working along with the energies of the Universe. It's only a question of effort to make this happen. In addition, each person has the moral responsibility to improve their character. It's a requirement for having a balanced life, but it goes far beyond that. Just think about your loved ones. Wouldn't you want them to live in a safe world and find their own happiness?

Good character is the key to successfully reaching divine enlightenment and unification with the essence of Olodumare, the ultimate destination of every soul. In the meantime, good character acts as a shield and guide, similar to Ori. Ori and Iwa work together to guide the soul on its path to fulfill its destiny in each lifetime. By working on both, your efforts and practices devoted to self-realization and spiritual growth will be more fruitful. Soon, you'll be able to enjoy the success you deserve.

# Signs of a Bad Character and How to Improve It

The ultimate goal of the Yoruba is to obtain Iwa-pele so they can reunite it with Ori and improve the latter. Both of these can be achieved by anyone. It only takes paying attention to certain actions and thoughts. This will enable you to start modifying them. You may be wondering how to tell if your character needs to improve. In order to answer this question, you'll need to look into your recent behavior. For example, if you're easily angered or provoked, you're quick to lose your temper and jump to conclusions without thinking things through, this indicates bad character.

Sometimes, bad character manifests in a way that makes you distance yourself from loved ones and the community. You can also feel the lack of inspiration to participate in spiritual gatherings and listen to your elders and spiritual leaders. You fail to devote time to prayers and other daily practices that promote a healthy spiritual life. If you're asked about this, you feel that you're being judged for not spending time cultivating your spiritual growth. You think that with so many things to do, it's not fair that you're being judged for missing a few prayers or rites. You can even start holding grudges against those who try to help you see the error of your ways. These will become triggers for sudden negative emotions.

There are also people with bad characters who feel trapped by unrealistic expectations or the need for dominance, limiting their own potential. When in fact, their options could be virtually limitless should they improve their personality.

You can also look into the character traits you have in your ancestral lineage. Sometimes, a bad character can be passed down in the family. This usually happens when one or more people fail to improve their personality, and the next generation learns their behavior. The bad character is repeated in the second or next generation, passed on to the third one, then the fourth, and so on.

Harboring negative thoughts about yourself can be another sign of bad character. While self-limiting and self-depriving thoughts can stem from traumatic experiences, cultivating them leads to even more misery down the line. Negative thoughts about others, including the feeling of superiority, also signify an unhealthy personality. Sometimes, people feel that they've reached a level of spiritual wisdom on which they can stop cultivating a positive character and start acting however they wish.

You can also experience losses, material, emotional and health-wise. Good luck will rarely be on your side if you're demonstrating bad behavior, but misfortune will definitely follow you.

If you've established that you need to improve your character, you can start working on this by learning about taboos and moral laws in your community. To further this development, look at moral expectations in broader society and learn how to respect them. Implementing certain acts of self-discipline is another way. For example, you can learn a few calming techniques if you have anger issues. These will teach you to think before you act or speak when you are angry, and you'll soon realize the benefits of not giving in to these disruptive emotions.

If your character issues are caused by unrealistic expectations (such as peer pressure and expectations from friends and family), the best way to tackle the problem is to counter them with positive affirmations. So, what if someone expects you to become someone you can't be? You've achieved many other things in life, so focus on these. If others can't see your success, this shouldn't be a problem for you. Remain gentle and kind to them. If their character is good, they will eventually understand. People with foul characters probably won't. However, since they have a negative influence on your spiritual energy, you should limit your interaction with them anyway.

Offering ebbos to Orishas and other spiritual leaders can also improve your character. You can ask your helpers for advice on removing negative influences from your life. Sometimes, appeasing a spiritual being alone motivates them to help you improve your character and Ori. Improving your character takes a lot of work. You'll need to arm yourself with patience while you're working on this. You'll need to be more tolerant of others and yourself too. You can ask your spiritual helpers for advice on practicing good behavior. This will enable you to become a valuable member of your community.

# Bonus: Glossary of Terms

Many of the terms relating to Ori and other Yoruba practices can be overwhelming and quite difficult to understand for someone who is just starting out. This bonus chapter will go over the Yoruba terms used throughout this book and is meant to make it easier for you. You can refer to it whenever you feel like you're lost.

**Ori (/ō.rí/):** Ori is a Yoruba metaphysical concept. The word literally means "head" when used in common language. However, metaphysically, it refers to a person's divine self, destiny, and spiritual intuition. It is the spark of human consciousness found in a person. Ori is often worshiped as an Orisha in its own right. When a person has a balanced character, they can align with their Ori. If a person dies before they can do that, they are reborn in their next life to try again. Mentioned in Chapters 1-10.

**Orisha (/ò.rì.ʃà/):** Orishas are spirits or deities that are considered to be emanations and emissaries of Olodumare. They are meant to assist humanity in living a successful life on earth. They are essentially the "gods" of the Yoruba pantheon. Mentioned in Chapters 1 and 4.

**Obatala (/ɔ.bà.tá.lá/):** Obatala is the sky father and the Orisha who created human bodies. He is also the Orisha of purity and is considered to be the father of all Orishas. He is the oldest Orisha and was the first to be created by Olodumare. He is also known as Orisa Nla and Oxala. Mentioned in Chapter 4.

**Esu (/è.ʃù/):** Also known as Eshu, Esu is the Orisha of duality, balance, trickery, chance, and the essence of fate. He is the divine messenger of the Orishas and serves as an intermediary between humanity and the Orishas. Mentioned in Chapter 4.

**Ogun** (/ˈəʊɡən/): Also known as Ogum or Ogoun, Ogun is the Orisha of blacksmiths, craftsmen, metalworkers, metal, iron, soldiers, and war. He is often associated with justice. Mentioned in Chapter 4.

**Yemaya** (/jē.mɔ̃.dʒā/): Yemaya is the Orisha of childbirth and water. She is known as the Mother of All Water and is considered to be the mother of all Orishas. She is the patron of the Ogun River and is one of Obatala's wives.

**Oshun** (/ò.sṹ/): Oshun is the Orisha of sweet waters, love, and beauty, as well as diplomacy and wealth. In one version of the Yoruba creation myth, it is Oshun who completed the creation of the world. She is the wife of Shango. Mentioned in Chapter 4.

**Shango** (/ʃà.ɡó/): Shango is Orisha of thunder and lightning, fire, and justice. He is a storm deity and is the strongest Orisha in the Yoruba pantheon. His wives are Oshun, Oya, and Oba. Mentioned in Chapter 4.

**Oya** (/ɔ.jā/): Oya is the Orisha of transformation, storms, thunder and lightning, and the wind. She is also the guardian of the dead and is a warrior Orisha who is said to be unbeatable. She is one of the wives of Shango. Mentioned in Chapter 4.

**Orunmila** (/ɔ.rṹ.mî.là/): Orunmila is the Orisha of wisdom, knowledge, divination, and prophecy. It is believed that Olodumare placed Ori in him, and he is the Orisha who can most affect a person's reality. It is believed that he once walked the Earth as a mortal prophet. Mentioned in Chapter 2.

**Ajogun** (/ā.dzo.ɡṹ/): Creatures that represent the negative forces of nature and are often associated with the Christian Devil. They bring misfortunes to people. However, they are not all evil and have some good in them. Mentioned in Chapter 1.

**Santeria** (/santeˈria/): Also known as la Regla de Ocha (the way/order of the Orishas), Regla Lucumí, or Lucumí, santeria is a religion that originated from Isese and developed in Cuba as a result of the slave trade. It is considered an African diasporic religion. Mentioned in Chapter 1.

**Voodoo** (/ˈvuːduː/): Also known as Vodoun and Vodou, Voodoo is a religion that developed in Haiti and traveled to the US as a result of the slave trade. It is a combination of several West and Central African religions, as well as Christianity. Mentioned in Chapter 1.

**Lwa (/lwa/):** Also known as loa or loi, lwa are spirits worshipped in Voodoo. They are similar to the Orishas in Isese. Mentioned in Chapter 1.

**Vilokan (/vilokan/):** Vilokan is the home of the lwas as well as the spirits of the dead. Mentioned in Chapter 1.

**Bondye (/bondye):** The supreme deity in Voodoo. Mentioned in Chapter 1.

**Candomblé (/kɛ̃.dõˈblɛ/):** Also known as Batuque, Candomblé is a religion that developed in Brazil but borrows heavily from Yoruba beliefs. It can literally be translated to "dance in the honor of the gods." Mentioned in Chapter 1.

**Ialorixá and Babalorixá (/ˈiyə.lo.riˈʃa/ and /ˌba.ba.lo.riˈʃa/):** Priestesses and priests in Candomblé. Mentioned in Chapter 1.

**Umbanda (/ũˈbɛ̃dɐ/):** A religion that developed in Brazil and is based on a combination of several African religions, Roman Catholicism, and several other beliefs. Believers of Umbanda worship the supreme deity Olodumareb or Zambia and also revere the Orishas. Mentioned in Chapter 1.

**Preto Velho and Preta Velha (/ˈpretʊ/ //ˈvɛ.ʎu/ and /ˈpre.tɐ/ /ˈvɛ.ʎɐ/):** Male and female spirits of the ancestors in Umbanda. Mentioned in Chapter 1.

**Iwa-Pele (/î.wà/ /kpɛ̀.lɛ́/:** The concept of having a good or gentle character. Mentioned in Chapter 10.

**Ifa (/î.fà/):** Both a Yoruba religion and a system of divination. Orunmila was considered the Grand Priest of Ifa. Mentioned in Chapter 9.

**Odu Ifa (/ō.dù/ /î.fà/):** Essentially a religious text comprised of 256 sections or odus. The knowledge of these sections can be transcribed into the 16 Truths of Ifa. Mentioned in Chapter 9.

**Egbe Orun (/é.gbè/ /ɔ̀.rũ̄/):** Also known as "heavenly mates." These are spirits who live in the heavenly realm. Each person has a heavenly mate, and these spirits guide and protect their twin in the human realm. Mentioned in Chapter 8.

**Eléékò** (/eléékòò/): An Egbe group that is led by their desires and whose mood is easily changed. Mentioned in Chapter 8.

**Ìyálóde** (/ììyálóde/): An Egbe group that are natural-born leaders. Mentioned in Chapter 8.

**Baálè** (/baálèè): An Egbe group that is a blend between Eléékò and Ìyálóde and has various personalities. Mentioned in Chapter 8.

**Asípa** (/asípa/): An Egbe group that is outspoken and vocal. They are often forgetful and disloyal. Mentioned in Chapter 8.

**Jagun** (/jagun/): An Egbe group that is highly adaptable and is identified with children who exhibit unusual behavior. Mentioned in Chapter 8.

**Olúgbógeró** (/olúgbógeróó): An Egbe group with a fluid nature and multifaceted personalities. Mentioned in Chapter 8.

**Móohún** (/móohún/): An Egbe group who are often childlike in their behavior and cannot be trusted with important tasks. Mentioned in Chapter 8.

**Adétayànyá** (/adétayànyáá): An Egbe group who revere refuse dumps. Mentioned in Chapter 8.

**Ibori** (/ibori/): A ritual that is practiced cleansing yourself and feed your Ori. Mentioned in Chapter 5.

**Odun Egungun** (/ɔ̀.dũ̀/ /ē.gũ̄.gũ̄/): Egungun are masked, costumed figures that represent the ancestors. Ofun Egungun are festivals that are held to celebrate the ancestors.

**Gelede** (/gelede/): A female masquerade held as part of Odun Egungun.

**Oso Ijoba** (/ɔ̀.ʃɔ́/ /i.dzo.bā/): A male masquerade held as part of Odun Egungun.

**Omiero** (/omiero/): Also known as purificacíon de santo. A sacred liquid that is used while conducting rituals. Mentioned in Chapter 5.

**Igba'Ori** (/ī.g͡bá/ /ō.rí/): A pot (sopera) that represents Ori. Mentioned in Chapter 5.

**Opèle** (/ɔ̀.k͡pɛ̀.lɛ̀/): A divination chain used in Ifa and Isese. Mentioned in Chapter 5.

**Ikin** (/ī.kĩ̄/): Sacred palm nuts that are used as divination tools. Mentioned in Chapter 5.

**Ori-Apere (/ō.rí/ /apere/):** Ori-Apere is a person's personal destiny. It also refers to a person's unique personal force or spiritual power and helps guide a person through physical and emotional challenges. Mentioned in Chapter 3.

**Ayanmo (/ayanmo/):** Ayanmo is a process by which people can get back in touch with the divine source and restore the balance of their body and mind. Mentioned in Chapter 2.

**Akunleya (/akunleya/):** Akunleya is the concept of being respectful while speaking, no matter who you are speaking to or what situation you are in. It is essentially speaking etiquette. Mentioned in Chapter 3.

**Akunlegba (/akunlegba/):** Akunlegba is the concept of transforming physically, spiritually, and intellectually to be well-rounded and develop a better understanding of oneself. Mentioned in Chapter 3.

**Babalawo (/bā.bā.lá.wō/):** Literally means "father of the mysteries." Babalawos are high priests of the Ifa oracle who perform various rituals and are believed to be able to tell the future of people who consult with them. Mentioned in Chapter 5.

**Ebbo (/e.ˈbɔ/):** Also known as ebo, these are sacrifices and offerings that are made to the Orishas, the ancestors, and other spirits. Mentioned in Chapter 10.

**Ori Inu (/ō.rí/ /ˈi.nu/):** The power of the mind, both physically and figuratively, in terms of power of thought and use of the mind. Mentioned in Chapter 3.

**Arugba (/arugba/):** Literally translates to "divine guidance." It is the external influences that benefit an individual – that is, the benefits they receive from being part of a community. Mentioned in Chapter 3.

**Ebo (/e.ˈbɔ/):** Literally translates to "exchange." It is the exchange between a person and the universe and refers to actions that affect a person's luck or fortune. Mentioned in Chapter 3.

**Iwa (/ì.wà/):** Literally translates to "character" in the Yoruba language. Mentioned in Chapters 3 and 10.

**Olodumare (/ō.ló.⁺dù.mā.rè/):** The Yoruba supreme deity. Olodumare is a genderless deity who is the creator of the world and the giver of the breath of life. They are also known as Olorun and Olofi. Mentioned in Chapters 2 and 4.

**Iwa-Buruki (/ì.wà/ /buruki/):** The concept of bad character. The opposite of Iwa-Pele. Mentioned in Chapter 10.

**Ise (/ī.ʃέ/):** Literally means "skill" in the Yoruba language. Mentioned in Chapter 10.

**Ogbon (/ɔ.g͡bɔ̀/):** Literally means "wisdom" in the Yoruba language. Mentioned in Chapter 10.

**Aiye (/aiye/):** A person's environment or the world around him. The word is also used to reference the earth or the physical realm (as opposed to the heavenly/spiritual realm). Also known as Aye. Mentioned in Chapter 10.

**Egan (/ˈiygən/):** The first wife of Orunmila. Mentioned in Chapter 9.

**Odu (/odu/):** The second wife of Orunmila. Mentioned in Chapter 9.

**Eji-Ogbe (/è.dzì ō.gbè/):** The youngest child of Orunmila. Mentioned in Chapter 9.

**Ife (/ī.fɛ̀/):** The place where humanity was born. It is also an ancient Yoruba city located north of Lagos in modern Nigeria. Also known as Ife-Ife. Mentioned in Chapter 9.

**Ofun-Meji (/ò.fṹ/ /médzì/):** One of the children of Orunmila. Mentioned in Chapter 9.

# Conclusion

The concept of Ori plays a central role in Yoruba beliefs and the practices of several other African Diaspora religions. Yoruba is a religion based on spirituality, where reverence for the soul is shown to both the living and the dead. According to them, the soul was given to living beings by Olodumare, which ensures its purity. Due to being preoccupied with mundane matters, spirits living on Earth have lost their connection to the divine essence they hail from.

Ori is a concept that encompasses the path to finding one's destiny and changing it if necessary. However, this is only possible if your values align with your Ori and if you have a sharp spiritual intuition. The concept of Ori is slightly controversial since it directly contradicts another fundamental Yoruba concept, the freedom of choice. However, Ori has several components and many forms, some of which make it possible to walk on the path of fate, all while maintaining and exercising free will.

The first step toward aligning with your Ori is to hone your spiritual intuition - as this is the part of you that lets you connect to the divine spirituality. One of the ways to do this is by calling on the Orishas, the divine messengers. The Yoruba believe that everyone has an "Orisha parent," but you can be guided by other Orishas too. In ancient times, people turned to Orunmila, a powerful Orisha and deity with divinatory powers. Nowadays, high priests and priestesses also perform prophecies to find a spiritual resolution to people's issues. Another reason venerating the Orishas can help you find your spiritual path is that Ori can also be viewed and honored as an Orisha.

Apart from honoring the Orishas and Olodumare, you can also work on your spiritual communication skills and awareness by remembering your ancestors. These wise spirits have a deep bond with you, which will come in handy if you struggle with awakening your spiritual intuition. If they see you have positive values that help continue their line, they will bestow many blessings upon you and your loved ones. Egbe Orun is another group of spirits you can turn to if you want to align yourself with your Ori. The Egbe has a tremendous influence over people's souls, but everyone should be careful when working with them. Some Egbe groups are easily angered and hard to placate. When crossed, they will retaliate by putting many obstacles in your path.

Odu Ifa, the ancient Yoruba prophecy, also plays a crucial part in spiritual fulfillment. It was created by Olodumare and given to the priests of Ife by Orunmila, who was entrusted with the resolution of conflicts and other issues among people. Since then, it has been passed down to the generations of high priests and priestesses of Yoruba, who learn to use its 256 signatures to guide, heal and support people in their communities. Odu Ifa can be summarized in the dogma named "The 16 Truths of Ifa." These truths serve as a guide to righteous living, which helps the Yoruba collect wisdom and reach spiritual enlightenment. Last but not least, you've learned that the ultimate role in improving and aligning your Ori depends on your personality. By improving your character, your values will become much closer to becoming an Ori representing that needed in order to live a fulfilled life.

# Here's another book by Mari Silva that you might like

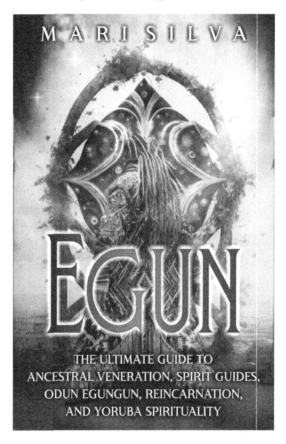

# Your Free Gift
# (only available for a limited time)

Thanks for getting this book! If you want to learn more about various spirituality topics, then join Mari Silva's community and get a free guided meditation MP3 for awakening your third eye. This guided meditation mp3 is designed to open and strengthen ones third eye so you can experience a higher state of consciousness. Simply visit the link below the image to get started.

https://spiritualityspot.com/meditation

# References

Africa Update Archives. (n.d.). Ccsu.edu. https://web.ccsu.edu/afstudy/supdt99.htm

Barrett, O. (2022, January 23). Voodoo: The revolutionary roots of the most misunderstood religion. TheCollector. https://www.thecollector.com/voodoo-history-misunderstood-religion/

Beyer, C. (2010, February 1). An introduction to the basic beliefs of the vodou (Voodoo) religion. Learn Religions. https://www.learnreligions.com/vodou-an-introduction-for-beginners-95712

Mark, J. J. (2021). Orisha. World History Encyclopedia. https://www.worldhistory.org/Orisha/

Murphy, J. M. (2022). Santería. In Encyclopedia Britannica.

Rudy, L. J. (2019, July 30). What is candomblé? Beliefs and history. Learn Religions. https://www.learnreligions.com/candomble-4692500

Asante, M. K., & Mazama, A. (Eds.). (2009). Encyclopedia of African religion. SAGE Publications.

AU press - digital publications. (n.d.). AU Press - Digital Publications. https://read.aupress.ca/read/sharing-breath/section/c53bd62e-abaf-4bd3-859d-20cf02db467a

Codingest. (n.d.). Orí: The significance of the head in Yoruba. Positive Psychology Nigeria. https://positivepsychology.org.ng/ori-the-significance-of-the-head-in-yoruba

Dopamu, A. (2008). Predestination, destiny, and faith in Yorubaland: Any meeting point? Global Journal of Humanities, 7(1 & 2), 37–39.

AU press – digital publications. (n.d.). AU Press – Digital Publications. https://read.aupress.ca/read/sharing-breath/section/c53bd62e-abaf-4bd3-859d-20cf02db467a

Balogun, O. (2013). The Concepts of Ori and Human Destiny in Traditional Yoruba Thought: A soft deterministic interpretation. https://www.academia.edu/3550807/The_Concepts_of_Ori_and_Human_Destiny_in_Traditional_Yoruba_Thought_A_Soft_Deterministic_Interpretation

Taiwo, P. O. (2018). Ori: The Ifa Concept of the Evolution of the earth. https://www.academia.edu/37623959/Ori_The_Ifa_Concept_of_the_Evolution_of_The_Earth

(N.d.-a). Researchgate.net. https://www.researchgate.net/publication/280495301_Predestination_and_Free_will_in_the_Yoruba_Concept_of_a_Person_Contradictions_and_Paradoxes_Philosophy_Culture_and_Traditions

(N.d.-b). Researchgate.net. https://www.researchgate.net/publication/237832774_The_Concepts_of_Ori_and_Human_Destiny_in_Traditional_Yoruba_Thought_A_Soft_Deterministic_Interpretation

A west African folktale of the story of oshún's flight to olodumare. (n.d.). Blackhistoryheroes.com. http://www.blackhistoryheroes.com/2015/10/a-west-african-folktale-of-story-of.html

An Illustration Studio. (2013). Creation Stories. Createspace.

Asante, M. K., & Mazama, A. (Eds.). (2009). Encyclopedia of African religion. SAGE Publications.

AU press – digital publications. (n.d.). AU Press – Digital Publications. https://read.aupress.ca/read/sharing-breath/section/c53bd62e-abaf-4bd3-859d-20cf02db467a

Hardy, J. (2022, July 2). 12 African gods and goddesses: The Orisha pantheon. History Cooperative; The History Cooperative. https://historycooperative.org/african-gods-and-goddesses/

Mark, J. J. (2021). Orisha. World History Encyclopedia. https://www.worldhistory.org/Orisha/

Ogbodo, I. (2022, March 17). Yoruba mythology: The orishas of the Yoruba religion. African History Collections. https://medium.com/african-history-collections/yoruba-mythology-the-orishas-of-the-yoruba-religion-f411c3db389d

Awakening to Your Divine Self: What is Ori Consciousness? (2017, September 20). Ayele Kumari, PhD / Chief Dr. Abiye Tayese. https://ayelekumari.com/ifayele-blog/awakening-to-your-divine-self-what-is-ori-consciousness/

How to align with your Ori? (n.d.). Infinity-Charm. https://infinity-charm.com/blogs/news/how-to-align-with-your-ori

Ibori – learn how to feed your Ori – babalawo Orisha. (n.d.). Babalawoweb.com.

Original Products. (2019, September 10). Creating an Orisha altar. Original Botanica; www.originalbotanica.com#creator. https://originalbotanica.com/blog/creating-an-orisha-altar-/

Ancestors. (2022, February 4). The Spiritual Community of the Òrìṣà - Energies of Nature. https://orisa.si/en/ancestors/

Egbe Òrun Complete. (n.d.). Scribd. https://www.scribd.com/document/494770885/Egbe-Orun-Complete

Egun / The ancestors - The Yoruba Religious Concepts. (n.d.). Google.com. https://sites.google.com/site/theyorubareligiousconcepts/egungun-the-ancestors

Isaad, V. (2021, October 23). Beginner's guide to spiritual practices to start connecting with your ancestors. HipLatina; HipLatina.com. https://hiplatina.com/connecting-ancestors-guide/

Baron, E. (2017, March 14). Beginning ancestor meditation. Nature's Sacred Journey. https://www.patheos.com/blogs/naturessacredjourney/2017/03/beginning-ancestor-meditation/

Connect. Collaborate. Express. (n.d.). RoundGlass. https://roundglass.com/living/meditation/articles/connect-to-your-ancestors

Evolve your ancestral story to heal & create change. (n.d.). Theshiftnetwork.com. https://theshiftnetwork.com/Evolve-Your-Ancestral-Story-Heal-Create-Change

How to build an Ancestor (Egun) shrine. (2017, September 20). Ayele Kumari, PhD / Chief Dr. Abiye Tayese. https://ayelekumari.com/ifayele-blog/how-to-build-an-ancestor-egun-shrine/

Onilu, Y. (2020, May 29). EGBE: "spiritual doubles" or "heavenly comrades." Chief Yagbe Awolowo Onilu; Yagbe Onilu. https://yagbeonilu.com/egbe-heavenly-mates/

Egbe Òrun Complete. (n.d.). Scribd. https://www.scribd.com/document/494770885/Egbe-Orun-Complete

Egbetoke, V. A. P. by. (2018, November 28). Ori, Egbe Agba, Egungun, Destiny, just to start knowing about. White Calabash. https://whitecalabash.wordpress.com/2018/11/28/ori-egbe-agba-egungun-destiny-just-to-start-knowing-about/

Ekanola, A. B. (2006). A naturalistic interpretation of the Yoruba concepts of Ori. Philosophia Africana, 9, 41+.

https://go.gale.com/ps/i.do?id=GALE%7CA168285830&sid=googleScholar&v=2.1&it=r&linkaccess=abs&issn=15398250&p=AONE&sw=w&userGroupName=anon%7Ed19920da

Fruin, C. (2021). LibGuides: African Traditional Religions: Ifa: Hermeneutics. https://atla.libguides.com/c.php?g=1138564&p=8384978

Made in United States
North Haven, CT
01 March 2025

66355045R00065